*Harvey Botchart is writing Grand Canyon Treks III, see p167, ~ 1985-1yr.*

# A Naturalist's Guide

## to

## Hiking the Grand Canyon

# A Naturalist's Guide
## to
# Hiking the Grand Canyon

by

Stewart Aitchison

PRENTICE-HALL, INC.                    Englewood Cliffs, N.J.

Prentice-Hall International, Inc., *London*
Prentice-Hall of Australia, Pty., Ltd. *Sydney*
Prentice-Hall of Canada, Inc., *Toronto*
Prentice-Hall of India Private Ltd., *New Delhi*
Prentice-Hall of Japan, Inc., *Tokyo*
Prentice-Hall of Southeast Asia, Pte., Ltd., *Singapore*
Whitehall Books, Ltd., *Wellington, New Zealand*
Editora Prentice-Hall do Brazil Ltda., *Rio de Janeiro*
Prentice-Hall Hispanoamericana, S.A., *Mexico*

©1985, by

PRENTICE-HALL, INC.

Englewood Cliffs, N.J.

*Library of Congress Cataloging in Publication Data*

Aitchison, Stewart W.
  A naturalist's guide to hiking the Grand Canyon.

  Bibliography: p.
  1. Hiking—Arizona—Grand Canyon National Park—
Guide-books.   2. Natural history—Arizona—Grand Canyon
National Park—Guide-books.   3. Desert survival.
4. Grand Canyon National Park (Ariz.)—Guide-books.
I. Title.
GV199.42.A72G733   1984      917.91'32'0453      84-15035

ISBN 0-13-610239-5
ISBN 0-13-610221-2 {PBK}

Printed in the United States of America

# Introduction:

# The Inverted Mountains

I was 14 years old the first time I gazed into the Grand Canyon. I could not believe the spectacle before me. There certainly was not anything like it back in the flatlands of Illinois.

"I want to go down there, Dad," said I, while pointing down toward the bottom of the great abyss.

"Maybe some other time," replied my father, secretly hoping that I would forget about such foolishness. We eventually returned home to the boring Midwest; my curiosity about the great Grand Canyon unsatisfied.

I began to haunt the local library in search of anything that had to do with the Canyon. I read James Ramsey Ullman's *Down the Colorado with Major Powell* and daydreamed over the historic photos in Lewis Freeman's *Down the Grand Canyon*. Roderick Peattie's *The Inverted Mountains: Canyons of the West* revealed just enough secrets of the Colorado Plateau country to whet my inquiring appetite. And then, in 1964, I came across a *Field & Stream* article penned by a Welshman who claimed to be the first man to have walked the length of the Grand Canyon. I read and reread Colin Fletcher's short piece, trying to imagine what it would be like to actually hike in the Canyon.

"Say Dad, aren't we going to Arizona next summer? Could we hike down into the Grand Canyon? Please?"

The next August found us on the Kaibab Trail heading toward Phantom Ranch. I am sure my father thought this trip would be nothing more than a long stroll. So did I. But the heat was oppressive, and our canteens were soon empty. Angry red blisters boiled up on our feet. (We each wore old street-shoes; I had never even seen a pair of hiking boots.) Cheap canvas packs hung like stones from our weary shoulders.

Somehow we made it to the oasis of Phantom Ranch. And after a refreshing dip in the creek-fed swimming pool (the pool was filled in 1972 for "sanitation" reasons), we felt revived enough to actually enjoy the evening light.

Very early the next morning, we started up the trail. All day long we sweated, panted, and dragged our tired bodies. At the end of each switchback, we would collapse and rest. Eleven hours later, we finally reached the rim, parched and exhausted. "I never want to go down there again," I swore as my leg muscles spasmed in pain. But Canyon dust was in my blood. I would be back.

According to a recent nationwide survey, many Americans believe that the Grand Canyon is somewhere in Nevada! Rest assured that the Canyon is still in northern Arizona.

To the majority of the annual 3 million visitors, the Grand Canyon means the South Rim—to them this Canyon extends from Desert View on the east to some 30 miles west to Hermit's Rest. Few tourists realize that they are seeing only one small portion of the 300-mile-long Canyon.

Many first-time visitors simply cannot appreciate the immensity of the Canyon. The mind turns off, a few snapshots are taken, and it's back in the car and another national park checked off the list. The average visitor spends a mere 20 minutes viewing the Canyon out of a total four-hour visit.

But for those who take the time to venture into the gorge . . .

In 1882 geologist Clarence E. Dutton wrote: "The Grand Canyon of the Colorado is a great innovation in modern ideas of scenery, and in our conceptions of the grandeur, beauty, and power of nature. As with all great innovations, it is not to be comprehended in a day or a week, nor even in a month. It must be dwelt upon and studied, and the study must comprise the slow acquisition of the meaning and spirit of that marvelous scenery which characterizes the (Colorado) Plateau country, and of which the great chasm is the superlative manifestation."

The Grand Canyon has been likened to inverted mountains. We peer not up to a summit but down into the depths. Exploration of the depths is limited to foot-travel except for mule-rides on the Kaibab and Bright Angel Trails and exciting whitewater raft trips down the Colorado. But the other trails, routes, and side canyons are accessible only to the walker, and then often only to the pedestrian well-versed in route-finding and climbing techniques.

This guide was written to serve as an *introduction* to Grand Canyon hiking. Walking the inverted mountains is uniquely different from most North American hiking—temperatures can be extreme, water can be in sight yet people die of thirst, trails disappear. This book has been divided into chapters covering the natural history, human history, canyon hiking information, and trail descriptions.

The approximately 30 trails included are by no means an exhaustive list. Rather these are a selection of routes of varying degrees of difficulty to introduce the backpacker to the Grand Canyon. Before venturing off on an extended hiking trip, you should test your stamina on one of the shorter, easier hikes. Also read up on the Canyon's geology. Michael Collier's *An Introduction to Grand Canyon Geology* is an excellent resource. Off trail route-finding in the Canyon is dependent upon a good understanding of the Canyon's rock layers.

Other guidebooks that you may wish to consult are Scott Thybony's *A Guide to Inner Canyon Hiking* and Harvey Butchart's *Grand Canyon Treks* and *Grand Canyon Treks II*. And if natural history is your love, take along a copy of Stephen Whitney's *A Field Guide to the Grand Canyon*.

Stewart Aitchison

# ACKNOWLEDGMENTS

I dedicate this guide to my father, Lawrence Aitchison, who unsuspectingly led me down the trail to my destiny. And to Bill Kemsley, who instigated this writing project and provided inspiration, guidance, and financial support.

Additionally, my appreciation and thanks go out to:

Harvey Butchart, who gave unselfishly of his vast knowledge of canyon trails and lore;

George Billingsley, geologist, who tried to teach me a little about the earth's history locked up in the Canyon's walls;

Mark Sinclair, Park Ranger, and David Maren, who both kindly reviewed the text.

Carol Woolery and Typing by JoAnn, both of whom translated my cryptic scribbles into legibly typed manuscript.

I gratefully acknowledge David Ganci for allowing me to quote from his *Hiking the Desert* and Alfred A. Knopf, Inc. for the quote from Colin Fletcher's *The Man Who Walked Through Time*.

Special thanks to David Hubbard for providing the original drawings. And finally to Ann and Bill, who continue to hike with me in spite of it all. Thank you.

*Stewart Aitchison*

# Contents

The Grand Canyon of the Colorado . . . is the most wonderful crack of the ground in America.

Dr. Elliot Coues, 1878

E. Mount Emma.
I. Inner Gorge.
P. Powell's Plateau.
T. Mount Trumbull.

1. Cherty limestone.
2. Upper Aubrey limestone.
3. Cross-bedded sandstone.

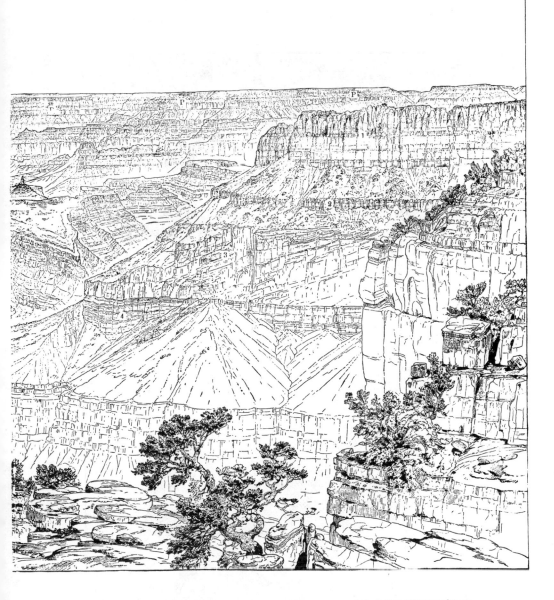

4. Lower Aubrey sandstones.
5. Upper Red Wall sandstones
6. Red Wall limestone.

7. Lower Carboniferous sandstones.
8. Quartzite base of Carboniferous.
9. Archaean.

## Point Sublime—Looking West

From John W. Powell 1895; *Canyons of the Colorado*. Reprinted by
Dover Publications, N.Y., 1961 under the title: *The Exploration of the
Colorado River and Its Canyons.*

**The Grand Canyon, Vishnu Temple**

From John W. Powell, 1895; *Canyons of the Colorado*. Reprinted by Dover Publications, N.Y., 1961 under the title: *The Exploration of the Colorado River and Its Canyons*.

# It Never Rains

We have rain from time to time all day, and have been thoroughly drenched and chilled; but between showers the sun shines with great power and the mercury in our thermometers stands at 115°, so that we have rapid changes from great extremes, which are very disagreeable. It is especially cold in the rain tonight. The little canvas we have is rotten and useless; the rubber ponchos . . . have all been lost; more than half the party are without hats, not one of us has an entire suit of clothes, and we have not a blanket apiece. So we gather driftwood and build a fire; but after supper the rain, coming down in torrents, extinguishes it, and we sit up all night on the rocks, shivering, and are more exhausted by the night's discomfort than the day's toil.

*John Wesley Powell, 1895*

One June sunrise found me camped at the mouth of the Little Colorado River. By the time the sun peaked over the east rim, the air temperature was 104°F (40°C). At high noon, the mercury in my thermometer (which was in the shade) was past the 120°F (49°C) mark and straining to go farther.

Fortunately I did not have to walk anywhere that blistering day. I alternated between lying in the cool waters of the river and sitting in the shade of a sandstone ledge.

In sharp contrast to the hot, dry month of June are the unsettled months of March and April. A couple of years earlier, spring had been exceptionally mild and promised inner canyon temperatures in the 80's and an early suntan. Long pants and wool shirts were left in the car. Down the Nankoweap Trail we blissfully sauntered wearing t-shirts and shorts.

The next day was windy and overcast. That night came the rain, which eventually turned into sleet. The following days vacillated between partly sunny to short snow squalls. Finally it was time to go home. We had only ascended a few hundred feet when all hell broke loose. It was snowing so hard that we could not find the trail. Our tracks were quickly covered by drifting snow. We only had shorts to wear and our legs were turning pink and numb. A retreat was in order. Back down we scrambled to the protection of a small cottonwood grove along Nankoweap Creek. The next morning dawned bright and crisp.

Never trust the weather. Always go prepared for the worst.

The average temperatures and precipitation for the rims and inner canyon are shown in Table 1. However, these are only a part of the weather story. The deviations from these arithmetic means are just as important to the Canyon hiker.

You may be misled into thinking that it is always warmer within the Canyon; and, generally, this is true. However, dense (thus heavier) cold air often drains into the Canyon at night. (This cold air drainage plays a role in "life zone reversal" where montane species of plants such as Douglas fir may grow at a lower elevation than one would expect. See the biology chapter for more about this phenomenon.) Additionally, during the winter months, the arc that the sun follows is so low in the southern sky that canyon bottoms receive minimal direct sunlight. At this time, inner canyon temperatures may actually be colder than the higher rims.

The fluctuation between daytime and nighttime temperatures can also be dramatic. The characteristically low relative humidity of the Southwest does not allow the air to retain heat. Once the sun sets, the ground and air quickly radiate heat out into the infinite heat-sink of space (unless there is a substantial cloud-cover to reflect this radiant energy). A 50-degree (Fahrenheit degrees) difference between day and night is not unusual.

"It never rains in the Canyon," is an often heard quote around these parts. But don't you believe it. There are supposedly close to 300 days of sunshine per year over the Canyon, but when it rains, well . . .

There are two rainy seasons—one from approximately December through March or April, the other usually extending from July until September.

The winter precipitation results from storms brought off the

**The Grand Canyon**

From John W. Powell, 1895; *Canyons of the Colorado*. Reprinted by Dover Publications, N.Y., 1961 under the title. *The Exploration of the Colorado River and Its Canyons*.

Pacific Ocean by westerly winds. If the storm originates in the Arctic, it tends to bring cold temperatures, winds, and little precipitation. On the other hand, if the storm is borne in the southern Pacific, temperatures will be milder but the clouds will be heavily laden with moisture.

During December of 1966, the North Rim received 14 inches of rain in 36 hours from a warm, tropical low. Bright Angel and Crystal Canyons were scoured by 40-foot walls of water. House-size boulders were pushed out into the Colorado, and Crystal Ripple was turned into the terrifying Crystal Rapid.

Occasionally one of these tropical storms will collide with an Arctic low over the Southwest, bringing heavy snowfalls. A series of such storms in December of 1967 buried Northern Arizona with over 6 feet of snow.

The North Rim, which is about 2,000 feet higher than the South Rim, normally receives an average of 200 inches of snow per winter. The North Rim road is often closed by mid-November and is not plowed until the middle of May.

Summer rains are derived from a completely different source. The winter westerlies begin to move northward during March. A high-pressure cell starts to build in the central and eastern United States and its clockwise circulation causes air to flow into Arizona from the southeast. By July this southeasterly flow is transporting moisture from the Gulf of Mexico into the Southwestern states. This moist air is pushed upward and condenses into clouds when it encounters the mile-high plateaus of Northern Arizona.

These clouds generally release their moistsure as short, afternoon thundershowers, rarely lasting an hour. The showers may be heavy "gully-washers" but typically bring less than .25 inches of rainfall. They are usually accompanied by a spectacular pyrotechnic display of lightning. The showers can be incredibly local. For example, in September of 1980, over an inch of rain fell in 20 minutes on Indian Gardens, yet only a mile away virtually none came to earth.

By September these moist southeasterlies are no longer entering the state, and autumn tends to be dry. But, again, autumn and spring defy generalizations.

Winds, of course, are associated with most storms, but uneven topography also affects local wind conditions. During the day, intense heating results in a strong rising of air along the canyon walls. Differences in temperature between the heads and mouths of canyons result in up-canyon winds. At night, the process is reversed as cooler air drains into the canyons.

Listen to "Cloudburst" from Ferde Grofe's *Grand Canyon Suite*. The musical mood darkens as black thunderheads fill the Canyon. The wind blows. Lightning streaks across the sky and rumbling thunder reverberates off the walls. And finally the cloudburst. Curtains of rain sweep across the chasm. Eventually the rain ceases but clouds still play in the Canyon. As the music reaches its climax, snow flies. Winter has come to the Grand Canyon.

Table 1

## GRAND CANYON NATIONAL PARK
## TEMPERATURES AND PRECIPITATION
(Fahrenheit and Inches)

| Average: | SOUTH RIM | | | NORTH RIM | | | INNER GORGE | | |
|---|---|---|---|---|---|---|---|---|---|
| | Max. | Min. | Precip. | Max. | Min. | Precip. | Max. | Min. | Precip. |
| January | 41 | 18 | 1.32 | 37 | 16 | 3.17 | 56 | 36 | .68 |
| February | 45 | 21 | 1.55 | 39 | 18 | 3.22 | 62 | 42 | .75 |
| March | 51 | 25 | 1.38 | 44 | 21 | 2.63 | 71 | 48 | .79 |
| April | 60 | 32 | .93 | 53 | 29 | 1.73 | 82 | 56 | .47 |
| May | 70 | 39 | .66 | 62 | 34 | 1.17 | 92 | 63 | .36 |
| June | 81 | 47 | .42 | 73 | 40 | .86 | 101 | 72 | .30 |
| July | 84 | 54 | 1.81 | 77 | 46 | 1.93 | 106 | 78 | .84 |
| August | 82 | 53 | 2.25 | 75 | 45 | 2.85 | 103 | 75 | 1.40 |
| September | 76 | 47 | 1.56 | 69 | 39 | 1.99 | 97 | 69 | .97 |
| October | 65 | 36 | 1.10 | 59 | 31 | 1.38 | 84 | 58 | .65 |
| November | 52 | 27 | .94 | 46 | 24 | 1.48 | 68 | 46 | .43 |
| December | 43 | 20 | 1.62 | 40 | 20 | 2.83 | 57 | 37 | .87 |

# A Sedimentary Journey

Time, geologic time, looks out at us from the rocks as from no other objects in the landscape. Geologic time! How the striking of the great clock whose hours are millions of years, reverberates out of the abyss of the past! Mountains fall and the foundations shift as it beats out the moments of terrestrial history. Rocks have literally come down to us from a foreworld. The youth of the earth is in the soil and in the trees and verdure that spring from it: its age is in the rocks . . .

Even if we do not know our geology, there is something in the face of a cliff and in the look of a granite boulder that gives us pause . . .

*John Burroughs, 1911*

The weather had been threatening all day. A light drizzle fell from steel-gray clouds. I crawled into the tent and snuggled into the warmth of my down-filled cocoon. I switched on my headlamp so that I could read *The Exorcist*.

The night grew even gloomier. Shivers of terror shook my body as I read the horror story when suddenly there was an explosion. I shot straight up in my bag nearly collapsing the tent. Silence . . . except for the wind gently flapping the tent walls. I sat down; I began to breathe again. Was I dreaming?

Boom! The hairs on the back of my neck bristled. Then the crash of tumbling rocks and then more rumblings and smashing noises. The grating of rock upon rock. Stones seemed to be falling out of the sky. The end of the world?

I cautiously peered outside, expecting to confront the devil himself. It was pitch black. All that I could see were snowflakes in the dim yellow light from my headlamp. The barrage continued throughout the night. I cowered in my sleeping bag; surely I would be dashed to bits by the hail of stones. "Oh, please Lord, don't let them get me. I promise to be good. No more picking the M & M's out of the gorp. No more hiking without a permit."

Slowly morning arrived and as the sun rose, the rockfall subsided. I ventured outside. The Canyon didn't look any different; the walls still towered thousands of feet above me. I had been spared.

Freezing thus expanding water had wedged rocks loose all night. Gravity did the rest. Yet the vastness of the Canyon hid the results. How many days and nights of freeze-thaw action does it take to widen the Canyon?

Ever since the first person gazed into the Canyon, people have wondered how it came to be. The Hopi, Paiute, and Pai people have their legends telling of the gods carving a "trail" through the mountains for great chiefs or heroes and then covering the trail with the raging Colorado to prevent others from following. Today's geologists have their stories about the Canyon's formation.

The backpacker in the Grand Canyon should study the various rock layers closely. Not only are they the key to unlocking many of the Canyon's routes, but they also tell an incredible story . . . the last 2 billion years of the earth's history.

Although most Grand Canyon hikes begin on the rim, and therefore you encounter the younger rocks first, this discussion will begin with the rock layers at the bottom. They are the oldest, and it will be easier to consider the geologic evolution in chronological order. Plus as you slowly plod up a steep trail, studying rocks is always a good excuse for a reststop.

Let's suppose you are at the foot of the South Kaibab Trail deep within the Inner Gorge. The towering black walls are composed of a rock called the Vishnu Schist. About 2 billion years ago, or roughly one-half of the total age of the earth, this part of the earth was a shallow sea. Volcanoes spewed ash and cinders. Lavas oozed up and out of great cracks, spread out over the land, and cooled to form basalt. Mud, silt, and sand were deposited in the sea. As these sedimentary layers became thicker and compacted, the mud and silt turned into shale, the sand into sandstone. For about 300 million years this accumulation of sediments continued.

Then forces deep within the earth began to uplift this region into a mountain range. The sedimentary and volcanic (igneous) rocks at the core of this mountain building were subjected to incredible pressure. Heat from friction and compaction was produced but the extreme pressure prevented the rock from melting. Instead the rock became pliable, the constituent minerals recombined to form metamorphic gneiss and schist, termed today the Vishnu Group.

**Rounded Inward Curves and Projecting Cusps of the Walls**
**(Canyon Contours)**

From John W. Powell 1895; *Canyons of the Colorado*. Reprinted by
Dover Publications, N.Y., 1961 under the title: *The Exploration of the
Colorado River and Its Canyons.*

As the uplift continued, magma (molten rock) was injected into cracks in the metamorphic rocks forming the pink streaks and bands of granite named the Zoroaster Granite.

At some point the rate of erosion of the mountain range outstripped the uplifting forces and by 1.2 billion years ago, the Vishnu Mountains had been worn down to a plain dotted with small hills. A shallow sea slowly invaded the area.

Sediments from some distant eroding highlands were washed into this sea. Four-hundred million years slowly, ever so slowly, ticked away. The layers of silt, mud, and sand accumulated to a thickness of at least 2 miles while keeping pace with the subsiding land. Magmas intruded these layers. The lavas pushed and melted their way between and through layers of sediment. One impressive lava dike can be seen across the Colorado river from the bottom of the New Hance (Red Canyon) Trail. Other billion-year-old lavas are exposed as dark-gray or black cliffs in Basalt Canyon near the base of Tanner Trail.

Shortly after 800 million years ago, this 2-mile-plus-thick sedimentary sandwich was broken by earthquakes that tilted the fragmented sections 10 to 15 degrees forming block-faulted mountains. The next 300 million years of erosion reduced these mountains into hills. The remnants of these tilted hills can be seen in eastern Grand Canyon from the Kaibab Trail east to the Tanner Trail and north to Nankoweap. Geologists collectively call the sedimentary rocks of these broken block mountains the Grand Canyon Supergroup. Each individual formation of shale and sandstone within the group has also been given a name. (See *Geology of the Grand Canyon* edited by William Breed and Evelyn Roat and Nankoweap Trail description for more details.)

Whew! Time to take a rest. You have passed through a billion and a half years of time and you are only a little over 1,000 feet above the Colorado River. Take a good long look at the Vishnu Group. You can see the bends and folds that took place so long ago as the layers of rock were squeezed and pushed around by the forces of mountain building. The wrinkles of age.

Now look at the upper layers of rock. See anything different about them? Right. All of the remaining formations (as each distinct layer is referred to) are nearly horizontal. They are in essentially the same alignment as when they were deposited as sediments.

The interval of time (about 300 million years of erosion instead of deposition) represented by the angular contact between the lower metamorphic rocks and tilted sediments and the upper horizontal layers of rock is called the Great Unconformity. It marks the end of the first chapter (The Precambrian Era) in our geologic story.

Okay, the reststop is over. It is now 550 million years ago and a sea is advancing from the west. There is something new and exciting in this ocean . . . animals with hard shells, similar to modern clams and coral. There are trilobites and worms, marine plants and snails.

The calcium carbonate derived from the shells of the new marine animals and calcium-rich rivers flowing from volcanoes inland would become the primary source for limestone deposition on the sea floor.

At the edge of this advancing sea, coastal sand dunes were flooded. Eventually silt and mud covered the sand as the shore moved eastward. As the sea continued to deepen, lime from the shells of countless generations of marine animals covered the mud. After about 50 million years, the sea began to regress toward the west.

The sand, the mud, and the lime layers are exposed today as the tan Tapeats Sandstone, the greenish Bright Angel Shale, and the gray to greenish-purple Muav Limestone.

After the sea regressed, the top of the Muav was exposed to erosion and several small drainages carved valleys into this stone. To the east, streams and rivers meandered across the surface flowing to the west where a shallow, highly saline sea still existed. The sediments deposited in the river channels and ocean became the Temple Butte Limestone. The river channel deposits are less than 100 feet thick and extend laterally only a few hundred feet at most; however, moving westward the ocean deposits accumulated thicknesses of more than 450 feet of limestone and silt.

Another long period of erosion followed producing another uncomformity. Then over several million years, another sea invaded the area, and a marine limestone was deposited. The purity of this limestone, the Redwall, suggests that streams and rivers rich in dissolved calcium carbonates derived from onshore limestone formations emptied into this sea. The calcium carbonate precipitated out on the ocean floor along with the shells of billions of sea animals, mainly plankton, and slowly accumulated to a thickness in excess of 500 feet in eastern Grand Canyon and 700 feet in western Grand Canyon.

The Redwall is gray in color, but the surface has been stained by red iron oxides that have washed down from the overlying Supai and Hermit formations. The Redwall forms the most persistent cliff throughout the Canyon. Even Harvey Butchart, the inveterate Grand Canyon hiker (see more about Butchart in the History of Canyon Walkers chapter), has found only about 154 places to walk through the Redwall Limestone cliff in its hundreds of miles of exposure.

Examine the Redwall closely. Marine fossils such as corals and brachiopods are common and crinoid stems ("sea lilies") are abundant.

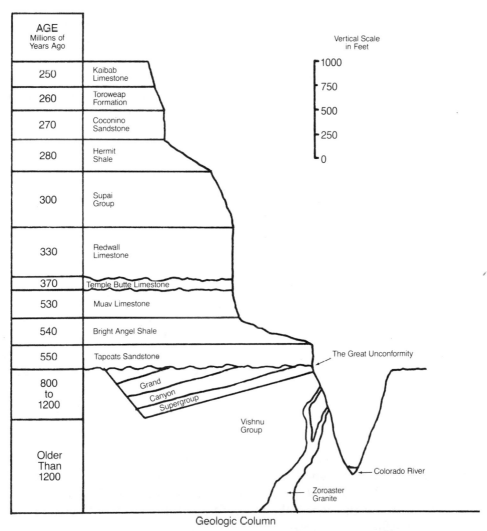

**Geologic Cross-Section of the Grand Canyon's Rock Strata**

Stewart Aitchison

The Redwall sea transgressed and regressed three times, depositing the thick sequence of limestone visible today. After the last regression, about 300 million years ago, this land was exposed to erosion to form another unconformity.

The next 1,000 feet of reddish-colored layers of rock are shales, siltstones, sandstones, and some limestone. The upper 300 feet of rock is a relatively soft shale and forms a slope. It is called the Hermit Shale. Below the Hermit is the Supai Group of formations. Because of its many beds of differing hardness and rock type, they form a series of ledges, cliffs, and minor slopes. The red color is caused by iron oxides. Fossil mud-cracks and fern leaves are indicative of a swampy, lagoon type of depositional environment.

The land rose and the area became covered with huge sand dunes. Today the wind-blown dunes are preserved as the buff, white Coconino Sandstone cliff overlying the red Hermit Shale. In the 300-foot cliffs, one can see the sloping layers of these dune sands where they form peculiar wedge-shaped patterns called cross-bedding. Fossilized reptile tracks found in this formation are almost always going uphill. Geologists devised many wild and ingenious theories to explain this curious phenomenon, including the suggestion that these ancient reptiles walked to the top of a dune and then were able to fly or glide to the bottom. An experiment with a present-day lizard solved the mystery. It was found that as the animal walked uphill, it left distinct tracks. As the lizard came down the dune, the downward momentum of the animal produced "blurred" tracks which became further filled with sand as the animal continued down the slope.

Eventually the Coconino Desert was covered by a sea and more sand and limestone was deposited. These marine sediments are today the 250-foot-thick, tan Toroweap Formation. There was a brief interlude of erosion when the sea regressed, then the sea returned and the Kaibab Limestone, a 250-foot-thick, ledge-and-cliff-former was laid down.

The regression of the Kaibab Sea marks the end of the second chapter (the Paleozoic Era) of the geologic history of the Grand Canyon area. Congratulations, you have reached the top of the Canyon although not the end of the story. We still have 225 million years to account for.

The next 150 million years (the Mesozoic Era) continued to experience a progression of seas, swamps, rivers, and deserts. More limestones, shales, and sandstones were formed. Dinosaurs ruled the earth. A sequence of rock, possibly as thick as 5,000 feet covered the Kaibab Limestone. But as a result of extensive erosion only scattered small remnants of these rocks are left at the Canyon. Cedar Mountain, near Desert View; Red Butte, south of Grand Canyon Village; and one small exposure near Rose Wells, south of the rim along the old railroad are examples. (Mesozoic rocks are more readily seen in nearby Zion and Petrified Forest National Parks, and around Lee's Ferry and Paria Canyon (Grand Canyon Trail #2).) End of chapter three, but still no topographic feature called the Grand Canyon.

About 65 million years ago (the Cenozoic Era), great forces deep within the earth caused 130,000 square miles of land known as the Colorado Plateau to be slowly uplifted. This huge block of real estate is on the average a mile above sea level and has been carved into a labyrinth of canyons, mesas, and buttes. This plateau is drained by the Colorado River and its tributaries.

As the Colorado Plateau was uplifted, compressional forces along its east and west flanks caused buckling of the rock layers into gentle folds that generally run north and south. These wrinkles may vary from small folds within one formation or stretch hundreds of miles and affect numerous formations. A good example of this latter type is the East Kaibab Monocline (monocline meaning "strata that dip"). Drive west on U.S. Highway 89A from House Rock Valley to Jacob's Lake. The road winds up and up. Look at the tilt of the rock layers, nearly vertical in places. This is the monocline. Another impressive monocline can be seen along the Grandview Trail (Grand Canyon Trail #15).

About 20 million years ago additional underground disturbances caused portions of the Plateau to crack forming joints, and in places there was up-and-down motion (earthquakes) along fractures which is called faulting. The rocks broken up by joints and faults were slowly removed by flowing water and wind. The Colorado River and its tributaries have carved downward into the Plateau while weathering forces such as frost-wedging, which I mentioned earlier, widen the Canyon. As geologist Michael Collier succinctly states in his book: "Weathering, erosion, transport."

How old is the Grand Canyon? Ironically perhaps more is known about the incredibly ancient environments that each rock layer was

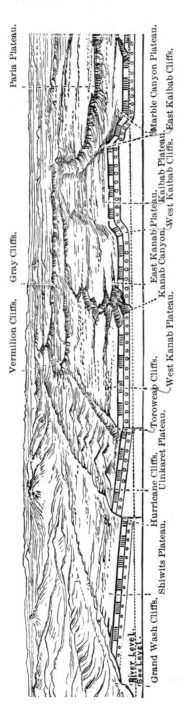

**Section and Bird's-Eye View of the Plateaus North of the Grand Canyon**

From John W. Powell, 1895; *Canyons of the Colorado*. Reprinted by Dover Publications, N.Y., 1961 under the title: *The Exploration of the Colorado River and Its Canyons.*

deposited in than the relatively more recent event of the carving of the Canyon. Radiometric dating seems to indicate varying ages at different locations.

Was the ancestral Grand Canyon really a series of canyons that later became connected? How did the Colorado River find a course through the 9,000-foot Kaibab Plateau? The geologists continue to ponder. The curious should read *Geology of the Grand Canyon*, edited by William Breed and Evelyn Roat for a survey of the current theories.

All that can be said for certain at this time is that the Colorado River has been eroding the Grand Canyon for at least 6 million years. A dab of icing was added to this geologic layer cake about 1 million years ago in the form of basaltic lava flows. Lavas poured into western Grand Canyon occasionally damming the Colorado River. Some tributary canyons have been completely filled in with volcanic material. Several striking examples exist in the Whitmore Wash area.

Erosion carved the canyon. Each rock layer has a different hardness and erodes in its own particular style. Harder formations tend to form cliffs; softer formations form slopes. This differential erosion has given the Canyon its distinctive stair-step profile. In the central section of the Canyon the resistant Tapeats Sandstone forms a relatively flat, broad surface called the Tonto Platform or Plateau. In western Grand Canyon the Esplanade Sandstone, a formation of the Supai Group, forms a similar platform called the Esplanade.

Tributary canyons whose downward erosion has followed joints tend to be zig-zag in course. Fault-controlled canyons tend to be straighter in line. The intricate dendritic pattern of washes flowing into canyons, canyons joining canyons, small canyons meeting larger canyons finally culminate in the grandest canyon of all.

To appease the geologic gods, I now faithly acquire a hiking permit, but I still pick the M & M's out of the gorp. And I have come to eagerly anticipate a "geologic event." But most of the erosional forces are so slow, in terms of human time, that to actually witness a rock fall or the scouring of a canyon by a flashflood is a real treat. The history of the earth is visible here for those willing to look. Feel the smoothness of polished schist and granite, the grittiness of the sandstone, or the sharp points on a chunk of weathered limestone. Look at the fossils, the first experiments with life. Listen to the wind, ethereal tales of the past. Hiking the Canyon is definitely " . . . a walk through time."

# Canyon Critters and Plants

We do not yet have a Grand Canyon between Shiva (Temple) and the North Rim, only a vertical interval of 1,300 feet . . . We did not expect to find Dinosaurs; we did not find them. We may have been several thousand years too early to find tangible evidence of evolutionary changes; these will most certainly appear sooner or later, with the setup such as that on Shiva, and I hope that they have already begun to appear.

*Harold E. Anthony, 1937*

It has been said that a trip from the bottom of the canyon to the rim is like a journey from northern Mexico to southern Canada. Considering the similarities in bureaucratic red tape involved in crossing borders and obtaining a park service hiking permit, I must agree.

However, the analogy was actually referring to the parallelism of plant communities. The bottom of the Canyon supports a desert community not unlike that of Sonora, Mexico. Ascending the Canyon walls, cooler temperatures and more rainfall allows a graduation from desert scrub to pinyon pine-juniper woodland and then to Ponderosa pine forest, and, at the higher elevations on the North Rim, spruce-Douglas fir forest similar to those found in northern climes.

One of the first to make scientific note of this phenomenon was biologist C. Hart Merriam. In 1889, Merriam, and his assistant, Vernon Bailey, were in northern Arizona obtensibly to shed light on the economic (primarily agricultural) importance of the biotic resources of an area encompassing a . . . "diversity of physical and climatic conditions, particularly . . . a high mountain . . . The San Francisco Peaks just north of Flagstaff were chosen because of their . . . southern position, isolation, great altitude, and proximity to an arid desert."

Their main camp was at Little Spring at the northern base of the San Francisco Peaks. On September 9, they headed toward the Grand Canyon following the "usual road." This two-day route went from Little Spring to Hull Spring to Red Horse Tank, and then to a tank known as Cañon Spring. From there Merriam and Bailey descended the Old Hance Trail and spent two days and nights within the Canyon. Merriam found the cactus mice "excessively abundant," adding later, "During the two nights spent in the cañon, these mice came about my blanket in great numbers and I was forced to place my scanty stock of provisions in a small tree for protection; but even there it was not safe, for the mice are excellent climbers, and I shot one by moonlight as it peered down at me from a low branch." Another night "I (Merriam) was awakened at midnight by a sniffling noise about my head. Rising suddenly on my elbow, a small animal scampered hurriedly away over the rocks. His form was only dimly outlined in the dark, but a hasty shot left no doubt as to his identity, and a moment later I held in my hand the type of a new species of little striped skunk." Other new species of plants and animals were collected during their stay.

The work done in the Canyon, on the San Francisco Peaks and the surrounding area eventually led Merriam to formulate his now famous Life Zone concept of plant and animal communities distributed on the basis of temperature. Along with this he noted that the unusual nature of varied climatic conditions of northern Arizona "bring into close proximity species characteristic of widely separated regions."

According to Merriam, in the Grand Canyon, you find the following Life Zones:

Lower Sonoran —characterized by the desert scrub

Upper Sonoran —the pinyon pine-juniper woodland

Transition —the Ponderosa pine forest

Canadian —the fir forest

Hudsonian —the spruce-fir forest

His so-called "laws of temperature control" supposedly governed completely the distribution of plants and animals. But it was not long before other biologists began to discover exceptions to the "laws." It is now accepted that besides temperature other environmental factors, such as moisture, contribute to determining plant

**Kanab Canyon, Near the Junction**

From John W. Powell, 1895; *Canyons of the Colorado*. Reprinted by
Dover Publications, N.Y., 1961 under the title: *The Exploration of the
Colorado River and Its Canyons.*

distribution. Also, although animals in many cases have specific food or shelter requirements that limit them to certain habitats, very few creatures are restricted to a particular Merriam Life Zone. In spite of the new theories, the contribution to the study of the ecology of northern Arizona and biogeography in general by Dr. Merriam is of lasting importance.

Since Merriam's Life Zones were developed for this area, you often see them still in use in many popular books and displays concerning this Canyon. However, today's Canyon biologists usually recognize seven major plant associations near or in the Canyon; namely, spruce-fir-aspen forest, mountain meadow, ponderosa pine, pinyon-juniper woodland, desert scrub, seep-spring-stream, Colorado River riparian. These associations correspond roughly with certain elevations but as with Merriam's laws there are exceptions. For example, just below the South Rim in protected areas, small stands of Douglas fir exist while on the rim is pinyon-juniper woodland. Fir is usually found growing at higher elevations but here on a shaded, north-facing wall, protected from drying winds and hot sun and where winter snows linger, this tree can grow well below its usual range.

> *Spruce-Fir-Aspen Forest:* On the North Rim, mostly above 8,200 feet, is found a spruce-fir forest intermixed with stands of quaking aspen. Englemann spruce, blue spruce, Douglas fir, aspen, and mountain ash are the predominant trees of this community. The forest canopy is dense and little sunlight reaches the forest floor. As a result, there are few herbs and grasses but more mosses and lichens. As mentioned before, some of these "high altitude" plants have found suitable niches for growth below the Canyon rim.

> *Mountain Meadows:* Scattered over the higher elevations of the North Rim are shallow, open valleys free of trees. Here a variety of grasses, such as mountain muhly, blue grama, black dropseed, and squirreltail, and herbs, grow. Along the meadow-forest edge may be found shrubs like currant, dwarf juniper, and cinque foil. Gentians, violets, and other wildflowers dot the meadows by late summer.

> *Ponderosa Pine Forest:* Between 7,000 and 8,000 feet are found extensive stands of ponderosa pine. The mature pine forest is fairly open which encourages the growth of grasses, shrubs, and wildflowers. Typical species include New Mexican locust, Gambel's oak, mountain mahogany, Oregon grape, buckbrush, wax currant, manzanita, sagebrush, cliff-rose, squirreltail, blue grama, as well as lupine, Indian paintbrush, fleabane, and sunflowers.

> Ponderosa is also found on top of some of the isolated buttes and mesas within the Canyon such as Shiva Temple and Powell Plateau.

**Scenery on the High Plateaus**

From John W. Powell, 1895; *Canyons of the Colorado*. Reprinted by Dover Publications, N.Y., 1961 under the title: *The Exploration of the Colorado River and Its Canyons.*

*Animals of the Forests and Meadows:* Associated with the forest and meadow plant communities are complementary populations of animals. Many animals move between two or more plant communities either daily while foraging or seasonally during migration. Nevertheless, there are certain groups or assemblages of animals characteristic of each major plant association. The only amphibians that could be considered typical of the coniferous forests of the Grand Canyon are the tiger salamander and Great Basin spadefoot toad. Both require ponds or rain-pools for breeding.

Skinks and garter snakes may be found in moist meadows. Short-horned lizards (also called horny toads), fence lizards, and gopher snakes frequent the drier pine forest.

Quite a few birds are typical of coniferous forests. They include:

> Turkey
> Great Horned Owl
> Saw-Whet Owl
> Broad-Tailed Hummingbird
> Common Flicker (Red-Shafted Flicker)
> Yellow-Bellied Sapsucker
> Hairy Woodpecker
> Olive-Sided Flycatcher
> Violet-Green Swallow
> Steller's Jay
> Clark's Nutcracker
> Mountain Chickadee
> Pygmy Nuthatch
> Brown Creeper
> Hermit Thrush
> Mountain Bluebird
> Townsend's Solitaire
> Ruby-Crowned Kinglet
> Warbling Vireo
> Yellow-Rumped Warbler
> Grace's Warbler
> Western Tanager
> Pine Siskin
> Green-Tailed Towhee
> Dark-Eyed Junco
> Gray-Headed Junco

Some of the mammals that are restricted, at least to some extent, to the coniferous forest are:

Dwarf Shrew
Long-Tailed Vole
Northern Pocket Gopher
Long-Tailed Weasel
Porcupine
Red Squirrel
Abert Squirrel—South Rim only
Kaibab Squirrel—North Rim only
Uinta Chipmunk
Golden-Mantled Ground Squirrel
Mountain Lion
Mule Deer

*Pinyon-Juniper Woodland:* Below 7,000 feet pinyon pine and juniper become the predominant trees. They grow along the rims, on some of the buttes and mesas, and down into the Canyon to the top of the Redwall Limestone. Other plants found in this woodland community include cliff-rose, broadleaf yucca, service berry, rabbitbrush, Mormon tea, sagebrush, fernbrush, Apache plume, buffalo-berry, hoptree, and blue grama grass. In well-drained, arid, rocky soils, the woodland may be intercepted with chaparral, which is a community composed of dense shrubs and stunted trees such as manzanita and scrub oak.

*Animals of the Woodlands:* Animal life of the woodlands is not highly distinctive. Most of the woodland species are also found in other habitats. Exceptions are the pinyon jay and the pinyon mouse which are fairly dependent upon pinyon pine nuts for food.

The western collared lizard, side-blotched lizard, fence lizard, and western whiptail are common. Some of the birds to be found include:

Mourning Dove
Common Poor-Will
Ash-Throated Flycatcher
Gray Flycatcher
Horned Lark
Scrub Jay
Pinyon Jay
Plain Titmouse
Common Bushtit
Bewick's Wren
Blue-Gray Gnatcatcher
Black-Throated Gray Warbler
Rufous-Sided Towhee

In addition to the pinyon mouse, woodrats, cliff chipmunks, and rock squirrels are found here, but any preference for woodland vegetation is superseded by the need for rocky hillsides and cliffs. Gray fox, coyote, mule deer, and an occasional lion may be seen.

*Desert Scrub:* Below the Redwall Limestone and extending down almost to the Colorado River is the desert scrub community. It is rather monotonous, botanically speaking, for it consists of only a few different species of plants. It is dominated by black brush, Mormon tea, several species of wild buckwheat, snakeweed, desert thorn, Utah agave, narrowleaf yucca, four-wing saltbush, various cacti, such as prickly pear, barrel, and hedgehog. These are species considered transitional between the Mohave Desert, which lies to the west of the Canyon, and the Great Basin Desert, which lies to the east and north.

*Animals of the Desert Scrub:* Many different kinds of reptiles make their home in the desert scrub including geckos, desert collared lizards, zebra-tailed lizards, and western blind snakes. Except for the tree lizard, side-blotched lizard, western whiptail and whipsnake, most are either uncommon or nocturnal, so rarely encountered by the hiker. One of special note is the Grand Canyon or Pink Rattlesnake. This is a unique subspecies of the prairie rattler that is only found within the Canyon. It is uncommon and shy and cannot tolerate hot ground temperatures. They range in color from buff-tan to reddish-brown and are usually less than 2 feet long.

Because of the lack of trees, birds of the desert scrub either nest elsewhere and only forage in this community or are ground or cliff nesters. The former include the turkey vulture, red-tailed hawk, golden eagle, and common raven. These birds prefer a cliff or large tree for nesting but spend a great deal of time hunting or scavenging in the desert scrub. Rock wrens and canyon wrens are commonly heard in the desert scrub.

One of the most prominent birds is the black-throated sparrow. It nests either directly on the ground or in a bush near ground level.

The mammals of the desert scrub include:

> Desert Shrew
> White-Tailed Antelope Squirrel
> Canyon Mouse
> Cactus Mouse
> Desert Woodrat
> Bighorn Sheep
> Black-Tailed Jackrabbit

*Seep-Spring-Stream Communities:* While the parched desert certainly predominates the inner Canyon area, scattered throughout the Canyon are small seeps and springs. Several springs are large enough to form perennial streams. In these wet places a myriad of water-loving plants survive, including redbud, birch leaf buckthorn, netleaf hackberry, squawbush, and poison ivy. Often maidenhair fern, crimson monkey flower, golden columbine, and the orchid helleborine are found. Vasey's Paradise, Fern Glen, and Elve's Chasm are but a few of these verdant gardens.

The dipper, black phoebe, and the canyon treefrog are restricted to these habitats. Many other animals must rely upon these places for drinking water.

*Colorado River Riparian Community:* This community is also the result of permanent water but differs from the tributary riparian (which means streamside) vegetation. Nor is the river community totally natural.

In 1963, the gates of Glen Canyon Dam, located just a few miles above the Grand Canyon, were closed. The wild and muddy Colorado (the river "too thick to drink, too thin to plow") became the tame and clear Colorado. No longer does the huge spring run-off from the Rocky Mountains make its way through the Grand Canyon to the Gulf of California. Before the dam, the run-off would scour out the Canyon, lay in new sand beaches, and remove and rearrange boulders brought in by side canyons. Even with the dam gates fully opened, only a fraction of the former volume of water is released, and it is clear; the sediment now collects in Lake Powell. [Note: *During the summer of 1983, record amounts of water were released from Glen Canyon Dam because of a heavy snowpack in the Rocky Mountains. Some scouring occurred but the ecological impact is still being assessed*].

Prior to the dam, woody plants were absent below the highwater line. This old riparian line is marked by the presence of shrubs and trees such as Apache plume, creosote, catclaw, and mesquite. Today the formerly barren beaches are being invaded by plants. To add injury to the already insulted ecology, the new shoreline community is composed mostly of saltcedar or tamarisk, an exotic species introduced into southern California in the late 1800's. Several native species, including coyote willow, arrowweed, and cattails are also coming in along the shore. It remains to be seen how this new community will develop as additional demands for the Colorado's water continues to grow.

Of the known 1,500 species of plants occurring in the Grand Canyon, over half grow within the riparian habitats. Clearly, water is the major factor in controlling plant distribution in the arid Canyon.

*The Riparian Animals:* Obviously the river is an extremely important source of drinking water for animals. Woodhouse's toads burrow into the sand during the day but hop down to the river's edge to sing and breed at night. Common animals include Lucy's warbler, Bell's vireo,

**Bighorn Sheep**

David Hubbard

blue grosbeaks, beaver, and white-footed deermice. In a few areas are also found river otters, ringtail cats, and raccoons.

The river, itself, is interesting biologically. Eighteen species of fish, 7 native and 11 introduced, live in its waters. The dam had a dramatic impact on the native fish that were adapted to breeding in warmer silty water. Many of these fish can now only reproduce at the mouths of the relatively warmer Little Colorado and Havasu Creek. For the backpacking fisherman (fisherperson?), there are rumors of big trout in Bright Angel and Tapeats Creek. A valid Arizona fishing license is required.

Besides Glen Canyon Dam, there are two other ecologically destructive forces at work in the Canyon that should be mentioned. First are the feral burros. Burros are cute but nonetheless exotic beasts in the Canyon, having been introduced by prospectors and other early residents of the area. They seem to eat everything in sight, which puts a real strain on the indigenous creatures. A very emotional nationwide argument ensued between the forces that wanted the wild burros left alone and the park service, who by law is mandated to remove exotic species from our national parks. The park service won out as of this writing (1984); it appears that most of the burros have been successfully rounded-up and removed from the Canyon.

This brings us to destructive force number two. It's you and me. There are simply too many people wanting to hike down into the Canyon. Hard to believe at first. The Canyon is *so* big! But over 80,000 overnight hiking permits are issued annually! The majority of backpackers use the easily accessible South Rim trails such as Bright Angel, Kaibab, Hermit, Grandview, Hance, and Tanner. The ecological impact these users have had on the Canyon has not been fully evaluated. But trampling of vegetation, increased soil erosion, population changes of certain species of insects, rodents and birds, and fouling of springs and streams are some of the problems. The chapter containing backpacking tips addresses human impact and what you as a hiker can do to mitigate disturbance of the Canyon environment.

Biologists have only recently begun to unravel some of the Canyon's ecological secrets. Virtually no biological research has been carried out on the Tonto Platform or the Esplanade. As recently as 1975, two new species of flowering plants were discovered along the river. As Merriam concluded in his 1890 report, *Results of a Biological Survey of the San Francisco Mountain Region and Desert of the Little Colorado River*, ". . . the Grand Canyon of the Colorado is a world in itself, and a great fund of knowledge is in store for the philosophic biologist whose privilege it is to study exhaustively the problems there presented."

# Bare Soles to Vibram

This region is, of course, altogether valueless. It can be approached only from the south, and after entering it there is nothing to do but leave. Ours has been the first, and will doubtless be the last party of whites to visit this profitless locality. It seems intended by nature that the Colorado river, along the greater portion of its lonely and majestic way, shall be forever unvisited and undisturbed.

*Joseph Christmas Ives, 1861*

There is an ancient Chinese classic entitled *Shan Hai King* written about 2250 B.C. that describes a voyage across the "Great Eastern Sea" and then a 2,000-mile journey in the land beyond. Some scholars believe that there are contained in this work accurate descriptions of American geography including the Grand Canyon, which is called by the narrator, "The Great Luminous Canyon."

It's debatable whether or not the Chinese were the first tourists to the Grand Canyon; however, by 2000 B.C. someone was venturing into the abyss and depositing small, animal figurines in remote, almost inaccessible caves.

These figurines were fashioned out of willow twigs. The twigs were first split lengthwise, then twisted and wrapped into deer- and sheep-like shapes. These figurines may have been used in a magical ceremony to insure a successful hunt.

Who these people were is lost in antiquity. Diagnostic projectile points (stone spearheads) found near the Grand Canyon suggest that these people may have been part of the Pinto Basin-Desert Culture, an enigmatic culture that hunted and gathered wild plants and wan-

41

**Split-Twig Figurines**

David Hubbard

dered the Intermountain West 25,000 to 8,000 years ago. These people apparently left the Canyon region by 1000 B.C. There seems to have been an hiatus of about 1,500 years before humans once again ventured into the Canyon.

These new people came to live and hunt within the walls of the Canyon about 500 A.D. Archaeologists recognize two different but similar cultures living simultaneously in the Canyon. In the eastern half were the Anasazi; in the western section lived the Cohonina. Neither had a written language (unless the pecked drawings and paintings on rocks these people left behind are some sort of hiero-glyphic language, an hypothesis rejected by most archaeologists). What is known about their way-of-life has been inferred from the remains of pottery, baskets, and other artifacts found scattered about the Canyon and assuming that their life-style was not too different from modern Hopi and other Pueblo Indians.

The Anasazi and Cohonina explored every corner of the great Canyon. Various routes were discovered through cliffs to go from rim to river. Some of these, such as the route off of the Desert Facade to the mouth of the Little Colorado, border on technical rock climbing. Many of the great buttes and temples were climbed and occasionally occupied, such as Shiva and Wotans. Most of these early trails were maintained through use, but in a few cases actual trail construction was done, perhaps a small retaining wall of stones or a propped-up log ladder. In Marble Canyon just a little upriver from President Harding Rapid is an Anasazi "bridge." It's perched high up in the Redwall and doesn't seem to lead anywhere. Perhaps it has some religious signifi-cance. Other trails go to springs and seeps and to mysterious caves where ochre, salt, and blue copper ore could be gathered for secret, magical ceremonies.

The well-dressed hiking Anasazi and Cohonina wore sandals to ward off the sharp rocks and prickly plants so common in the Canyon. These sandals were of two types. Yucca leaves were woven together to form a wickerwork sandal. Often the leaf ends were left loose except at the heel which provided a decorative fringe and extra pad-ding for the sole. The other type of sandal was woven from cord made from the fibers of the yucca leaf. These sandals sometimes had intri-cate designs.

Of the over 2,000 known sites in the Canyon perhaps 1,500 were inhabited between 1050 and 1150 A.D. But by 1150 A.D., these people abandoned the Canyon for reasons not yet fully understood. Some plausible theories are that the natural resources were danger-ously overused and there was a drying trend which made agriculture more tenuous in an already harsh environment. Most of these peo-ple probably were incorporated into the Hopi and the Pueblo cul-tures to the east.

About 1300 A.D. Cerbat Indians, ancestors of the present-day Hualapai and Havasupai, began to enter the Canyon from the lower Colorado River Valley. They spread as far east as the Little Colorado River but stayed primarily south of the Colorado. Their homes were

**Basketry**

From John W. Powell, 1895; *Canyons of the Colorado*. Reprinted by Dover Publications, N.Y., 1961 under the title: *The Exploration of the Colorado River and Its Canyons.*

**Ancient Pottery**

From John W. Powell, 1895, *Canyons of the Colorado*. Reprinted by
Dover Publications, N.Y., 1961 under the title: *The Exploration of the
Colorado River and Its Canyons.*

**Paiute**

From John W. Powell, 1895; *Canyons of the Colorado*. Reprinted by
Dover Publications, N.Y., 1961 under the title: *The Exploration of the
Colorado River and Its Canyons.*

circular brush wickiups; and instead of sandals, they wore leather
moccasins. They discovered new routes and reused the faint Anasazi
and Cohonina trails.

Meanwhile Southern Paiutes made seasonal trips to the North
Rim-Kaibab area to hunt deer and gather wild plants. The Paiutes
would occasionally cross the Colorado and raid the Cerbats. The Cerbats would also cross the river to retaliate. One possible route that has
been suggested is via Mohawk and Stairway Canyons in western
Grand Canyon.

Today the Southern Paiutes live on a small reservation north of the Canyon. The Hualapais live along the South Rim in western Grand Canyon; and the Havasupais live within the depths of Havasu (Cataract) Canyon. Moccasins have given way to cowboy boots and tennis shoes.

The prehistoric period ended in 1540 when Spanish conquistador Garcia Lopez de Cardenas spent three days searching for a way into the Canyon. Ironically, he and his men had been led to the Canyon's rim by Hopi, who, of course, knew many ways into the Canyon but did not reveal this knowledge. At least since the 14th century, Hopi had descended into the Canyon to gather sacred salt and other magical substances. Perhaps the Hopi were hoping that the white strangers would become discouraged and go away. The Spaniards could not find a way down and left.

Another group of native Americans, the Navajo, reached the Grand Canyon country sometime in the late 18th century but rarely descended into the abyss. Some Navajos may have hidden in the Canyon in 1863 while Christopher "Kit" Carson was attempting to incarcerate this tribe.

**A Navajo Hogan**

From John W. Powell, 1895; *Canyons of the Colorado*. Reprinted by Dover Publications, N.Y., 1961 under the title: *The Exploration of the Colorado River and Its Canyons.*

Today the Navajo Nation abuts the eastern boundary of the Park along Marble Canyon.

Over 200 years would pass before white men would again visit the Canyon. On the 20th of June in the fateful year 1776 a Franciscan missionary named Francisco Tomas Garces entered the "Rio Jabesua" (Havasu Canyon) via a wooden ladder fastened to a cliff-face in Hualapai Canyon. Garces named the muddy river the "Rio Colorado" and the great Canyon "Puerto de Bucareli" (Bucareli's Pass). Bucareli was a viceroy of New Spain.

During the last quarter of the 18th century and the first half of the 19th, there is precious little documentation concerning human activities within the Grand Canyon. Trapper-explorer James Ohio Pattie may have seen the Canyon in 1826, but his diary is so vague it is difficult to decipher locations. Other mountain men and trappers penetrated the region but left few written records.

In 1851 guide Antoine Leroux warned Captain Lorenzo Sitgreaves not to follow down the Little Colorado River Gorge because of obstacles in its lower reaches. Presumably Leroux was familiar with at least parts of the Grand Canyon. Seven years later, Lieutenant Joseph Ives descended Diamond Creek to the Colorado. The two expedition artists, F.W. von Egloffstein and H.B. Mollhausen, produced the first sketches of the Grand Canyon. Later the expedition traveled eastward to Havasu Canyon and von Egloffstein started down the same route that Garces had followed 82 years before. While on the ladder, a rung broke, and von Egloffstein was "precipitated into the abyss." He was unhurt and went on and visited with the Havasupai. Upon his return, he was pulled out of the canyon with gun slings tied together.

In 1869 geologist John Wesley Powell made his historic river run down the Colorado from Green River, Wyoming to the foot of the Grand Canyon. The hardships and toils of the raging river left little time for exploration away from the water's edge. Near the end of the river trip, three of Powell's men left the expedition and discovered a route to the rim via Separation Canyon. Unfortunately they were killed by Indians.

The following year Jacob Hamblin, a missionary for the Latter-day Saints, and Chuarrumpeak, a Paiute chief, located trails and springs in the Grand Canyon region to help Powell's further scientific studies of the Colorado Plateau and to further Mormon Settlement.

**Powell Boat Wreck**

From John W. Powell, 1895; *Canyons of the Colorado*. Reprinted by
Dover Publications, N.Y., 1961 under the title: *The Exploration of the
Colorado River and Its Canyons.*

After Powell's initial river trips, other geologists came to study
the rocky landscape of northern Arizona. Clarence Dutton's *Tertiary
History of the Grand Canon District* (1882) is considered a classic

geologic report. In it, Dutton states that there are only four trails leading from rim to river in the Canyon. (Today over 105 routes are known.)

The last 30 years of the 19th century saw an ever increasing amount of exploitation of the Canyon's resources. Timber was lumbered on the Rims, grazing of livestock occurred both within the Canyon and on the Rims, and prospectors, such as Seth Tanner and Louis Boucher, searched for gold and silver but found copper and asbestos.

By 1883, hardy tourists were bouncing in a wagon from Peach Springs to the bottom of the Grand Canyon at Diamond Creek. The next year, a Mrs. Ayer became the first (non-native American) woman to descend into the Grand Canyon. She walked down prospector John Hance's trail below Horseshoe Mesa.

Some prospectors found more riches in the tourist business than in the Canyon's minerals. John Hance, William Bass, Peter Berry, and Ralph Cameron developed their mining trails into riding and walking trails for Canyon visitors. (See the individual trail descriptions for more details.)

Some of the more notable tourists included General John J. Pershing. He visited the Canyon in 1889 when he was a 29-year-old second lieutenant. He and three friends became lost and would have died of thirst except a Havasupai found them and led them to Hance's ranch. Pershing would later remark that the Grand Canyon would make a great border between France and Germany.

In 1909, pioneer conservationist John Muir and naturalist John Burroughs descended the Bright Angel Trail, pausing near the top to have their pictures taken by the Kolb Brothers.

Emery and Ellsworth Kolb built a studio on the very edge of the South Rim at the head of the Bright Angel Trail in 1904. These photographer-explorers photographed mule riders on the Bright Angel for profit and made photographic sojourns into the Canyon when time permitted. Until his death in 1976, Emery showed his 1911 film of a Colorado River trip daily to South Rim tourists.

Up until the 1960's there were few people interested in hiking the Canyon for pure pleasure. Most of these early backpackers were rangers or local residents. A few came from more distant places and occasionally were climbers. One famous climbing expedition took place in 1937.

The American Museum of Natural History was interested in

finding out whether or not unique animals lived on the canyon's isolated buttes. An alpine guide was hired to lead the scientists to the top of Shiva Temple. The newspapers began to exaggerate the purpose of the trip, even suggesting that the expedition was in search of dinosaurs. The scientists found the animals on Shiva to be no different than those on the nearby canyon rim.

Probably the most famous hiker is Colin Fletcher, who in 1963, walked from Havasu Canyon east to the Little Colorado, swam across the Colorado, and exited via the Nankoweap Trail. He described his epic journey in *The Man Who Walked Through Time*. Another book, *The Complete Walker*, assured Fletcher's place as the nation's hiking guru. Backpacking became "the thing" to do in the late 60's and its popularity shows no waning.

But Fletcher had not done his Canyon treak trusting blind fate and sturdy legs. He sought out all the information he could find about inner canyon hiking. He talked to rangers, packers, geologists, and river guides. "But before long, it dawned on me that when it came to extensive hiking in remote parts of the Canyon, none of them really knew what he was talking about. So I set about tracking down the experts on foot travel. In the end I discovered that they totalled one: a math professor at Arizona State College in Flagstaff. But Dr. Harvey Butchart, I was relieved to find, knew exactly what he was talking about."

In 1945, Harvey Butchart came to Arizona State College (now Northern Arizona University) to begin a teaching career and hiked into the Grand Canyon for the first time. As a mathematician would, Butchart began a systematic exploration of the inner Canyon. First came the actively used trails, then the old, abandoned trails, and finally cross-country hiking and climbing routes. Of the 150 named temples, Butchart has scaled over half of them, about 50 being first ascents. He reconnoitered routes from small aircraft, talked with old Havasupais, gleaned historic books, journals, photographs, and maps for information. Now retired from teaching but not from hiking, Butchart knows more about Grand Canyon trails than anyone else alive today. His two little guide books *Grand Canyon Treks* and *Grand Canyon Treks II* are a wealth of information. But one word of caution, Butchart is a master of understatement. What he calls a moderate scramble may be a class 5 rock climb for some and his time extimates I usually multiply by 2 or 3.

Today, the popularity of hiking has necessitated a permit system

*My only experience- clear creek down to Colorado R was a great overstatement of the difficulty, the Chockstone was nothing !*

to mitigate overuse. But once you have broken in your boots on the easier trails, you can head off into the more remote sections of the Park. There may even be a few places left where Butchart hasn't been . . . yet.

**The Rescue**

From John W. Powell, 1895; *Canyons of the Colorado*. Reprinted by Dover Publications, N.Y., 1961 under the title: *The Exploration of the Colorado River and Its Canyons*.

# Planning Your Backpack Trip

The Grand Canyon is not the place for one's first experience in hiking.

*Harvey Butchart, 1970*

I am assuming you are an experienced hiker. If not, stick with strolls along the rim or day-hikes down the Bright Angel, Kaibab, or Hermit. Doing an overnight backpack with new boots, soft feet, and a 50-pound pack is no way to introduce yourself to hiking or the Canyon. Read up on proper technique; try Dave Ganci's *Hiking the Desert*—and, if possible, try some easier terrain first. Or you may opt for a guided trip. Contact Grand Canyon Trail Guides, P.O. Box 735, Grand Canyon, AZ 86023; (602) 638-2391 for more information and rates.

For those of you well-versed in the ways of the desert, familiar with the primitive activity of walking, and eager to hit the trail, I will mention in this chapter a few suggestions that hopefully will add to the enjoyment of your trip and the protection of the environment.

Canyon hiking differs from most in that first comes the knee-wrenching, ankle-twisting downhill trot. Then, once you are near exhaustion, commences the unbelievable uphill grind. The better physical condition you are in, the more enjoyable will be your trip.

Plan to take twice as long to ascend as it took to descend. This is often overlooked by the first-timer in the Canyon and can result in stumbling toward the rim or over a cliff in darkness.

Know how to read a topographic map. Although not critical on the busy South Rim trails, maps become increasingly important on the more remote, infrequently used routes. The appropriate maps are listed with each trail description. U.S. Geological Survey Topo Maps

...e available from the U.S.G.S., Box 25268 Federal Center, Denver, CO 80225.

Another good series of maps are being published by Rainbow Expeditions, 915 S. Sherwood Village Drive, Tucson, AZ 85710. These maps are called Grand Canyon Recreational Maps and utilize U.S.G.S. Topo Sheets as a base. Then they show, in contrasting colors, trails, routes, and points of interest.

The Grand Canyon Natural History Association has printed two geologic maps that cover most of the Canyon. These maps are very helpful in identifying the various rock layers and in route finding. The GCNHA's address is P.O. Box 399, Grand Canyon, AZ 86023. They also put out a series of books and pamphlets dealing with the Canyon.

For the map connoisseur, I should mention some other maps. One published by the National Geographic Society is called *The Heart of the Grand Canyon* and is available from the GCNHA. It is the most detailed map ever produced on the Grand Canyon. It covers the same area as the U.S.G.S. Bright Angel quad but at nearly three times the scale.

The other maps are out-of-print but may be found in some libraries. These are the historic Francois Matthes' maps. The Vishnu, Bright Angel, and Shinumo quadrangles were finished in 1905, and the remaining areas in 1920–1923 by Richard Evans. These maps are not only accurate but incredible works of art.

PERMITS *are required* for overnight hikes in the park and for *any* travel on Indian reservations. Each trail description lists who has jurisdiction over that particular section of the Canyon.

For park service permits, contact the Backcountry Reservation Office, Box 129, Grand Canyon, AZ 86023; (602) 638-2474, answered only 1–5 p.m. MST. Writing for a permit is more effective than phoning. These permits are free. However, due to high demand, reservations are recommended and should be made up to three months in advance of your trip.

For Havasupai permits write or call the Havasupai Tribal Enterprises, Supai, AZ 86435; (602) 448-2121. These permits cost money.

For Hualapai permits, contact Director, Hualapai Wildlife and Outdoor Recreation Dept., P.O. Box 216, Peach Springs, AZ 86434; (602) 769-2227. There is a charge. I have not had much luck with written correspondence. Usually it is best to call and/or drop in at their office in Peach Springs.

For Navajo permits, try the Parks Branch or Recreational Resources Dept., Window Rock, Navajo Nation, AZ 86515. I must admit that I have never been successful in obtaining such a permit but have found the Navajo people quite friendly if rather amused by Anglo-hikers. I'm sure the permit system will eventually be enforced as increasing numbers of non-Indians explore the reservation.

What to take? Your single heaviest and most important item is water. During the summer, plan to carry a minimum of 1 gallon per person per day. There are few permanent streams and few reliable springs. Park Rangers can assist you in locating water sources when you acquire your permit. Many of the Canyon's water sources have been contaminated by unthinking people with fecal coliform bacteria and/or the protozoan called giardia, so always purify drinking water—even the Colorado River. Be careful not to add to this problem by being careless with soap, food scraps, or human waste. Wash your body and dishes well away from water sources. Discard waste water over vegetation.

No open fires are permitted due to lack of wood and fire danger, so take a lightweight backpacking stove. If you miss a campfire, try a surrogate campfire by using a candle and a windscreen made out of aluminum foil.

A thicker-than-usual sleeping pad may be worthwhile since many campsites feature rock beds. A blanket will suffice during the summer but a warm sleeping bag is necessary in the winter when the temperature may dip to 0°F.

Desert soils are extremely friable. They are held together by specially adapted mosses and lichens which appear as black dots on the surface. A single footstep can wipe out several hundred years' worth of soil stabilization. Stay on trails or try to walk on rock surfaces or sand. Avoid campsite "improvements" such as trenching or building of rock walls.

Human waste decomposes very slowly in this arid climate. Choose a location at least 200 feet from water, trails, and campsites. Dig a small hole in topsoil about 4 to 6 inches deep. Make your deposit and cover it with soil. Pack out your toilet paper in a plastic bag. Do not bury it or burn it. Toilet paper "flowers" last for years, and tragic toilet paper fires have burned Deer Creek, Nankoweap, and other beautiful areas.

Consider Dave Ganci's suggestion, "When you get the call, simply gather a collection of small stones, twigs, dried plant material, grasses if available, and leaves if you know what they are. After mak-

**Fire in Camp**

From John W. Powell, 1895; *Canyons of the Colorado*. Reprinted by
Dover Publications, N.Y., 1961 under the title: *The Exploration of the
Colorado River and Its Canyons.*

ing your deposit and using your little pile of natural aids, push the soil
over the hole and walk away. Voila! No toilet paper to burn or to be
dug up by desert dwellers."

When camping along the Colorado River, remember that the
beaches are seldom cleansed by rainfall or the regulated river. Uri-
nate directly in wet sand at the river's edge (normal urine does not
contain bacteria). To defecate, walk above the beach area to a location
with soil and away from campsites. There are few decomposing bacteria in beach sand.

Respect the rights of the animals and plants that you encounter.
This is their home. Don't pick wildflowers. Don't kill snakes or any
other creature. Rattlesnakes are almost never aggressive. Just give
them plenty of room. Don't reach under rocks or into crevices and
you will virtually eliminate the chances of being stung by a scorpion
or bitten by a black widow spider.

Remember that the prehistoric Indian Ruins and historic mining
camps that you may happen upon can never be replaced. Do not
disturb their remains nor collect souvenirs so that future visitors and
archaeologists can enjoy and study them.

## Hazards

Never swim in the Colorado River. Many hikers have drowned because they underestimate the river's currents and bitter cold (45°–50°F) temperature.

Be careful when scrambling around on rock. Sedimentary rocks easily dislodge and handholds break off.

The tops of trails are often extremely icy in winter. In-step crampons may be helpful. Also heavy snows can obscure already faint trails. Know your route.

If you become lost, stay put. Carry a signal mirror and know how to use it. If you have obtained a permit and fail to return for your requested check-in, a search party will come looking for you. On Indian land this may not be the case; tell a friend where you are going and when to expect you.

Dying of thirst is a very real possibility. Carry the recommended 1 gallon per day per person. Increase your intake of salts through drinks (i.e., Gatorade) and food (gorp, nuts). Know the symptoms of heat exhaustion, sunstroke, and heat cramps. Do not rely on springs shown on the maps. Get current information from the National Park Service. If possible, hike the Canyon in the spring, fall, or winter. Avoid the summer heat and the crowds.

Prevention is much easier than treatment in the field. Take a first-aid course and read and reread a good first-aid manual such as James Wilkerson's *Medicine for Mountaineering*.

From blistering heat to frigid cold, to dying of thirst, to being run down by a flashflood, the Canyon offers plenty of dangers, but a careful, experienced hiker should have no problem. Do not overextend yourself—and, most of all, be gentle to the Canyon.

# Trails and Scrambles

In leaving the upper section of the Mystic Spring Trail (South
Bass), we had to descend, for perhaps two thousand feet, an
almost precipitous talus, with no suggestion of a trail. Now we
were dropping down eight and ten feet ledges, then climbing
over loose boulders, only to alight on a mass of sliding debris
which carried us along perilously near a precipice five hundred
feet high, over which we could hear the fore-portion of our
rocky stream fall upon the marble beneath. Several times we
found ourselves on ledges which ended nowhere, and our stops
had to be retraced.

George Wharton James, 1900

The following section contains over 30 possible hik-
ing trips into the Grand Canyon. Each trail description includes information on how to locate the trailhead (sometimes an adventure in
itself), approximate length, and difficulty of the hike. Rating the difficulty of each trail can be very subjective. Nearly all the routes described have the objective dangers of loose rocks to trip over, plenty
of sheer cliffs to fall over, and more than enough sun to bake your
brains. But what is an easy, hands-in-the-pockets stroll for one person
may be a terrifying adventure for the next. My advice is if you have
not hiked in the Grand Canyon before, choose a trip rated easy for
your first experience or do only a portion of a moderate trip. Save
those marked difficult until you are familiar with the Canyon and your
ability.

The trail descriptions are *not* painstakingly detailed, rock-by-
rock discourses on each route. I assume the user of this guidebook can
read a topographic map, has had some previous hiking experience,
and doesn't need nor want to be led by the hand down the trail. There
are hundreds, perhaps thousands, of possible hiking and climbing

**The Brink of the Inner Gorge**

From John W. Powell, 1895; *Canyons of the Colorado*. Reprinted by
Dover Publications, N.Y., 1961 under the title: *The Exploration of the
Colorado River and Its Canyons*.

routes within the vastness of the Grand Canyon. This guidebook is
simply a beginning point for Canyon exploration. Test your legs and
hiking skills on some of these trails, then go off and discover your own
routes.

Remember, trail conditions may change through time—
especially access routes to trailheads. Please send any corrections of
trail descriptions or comments to me in care of the publisher. Thanks,
and Happy Hiking!

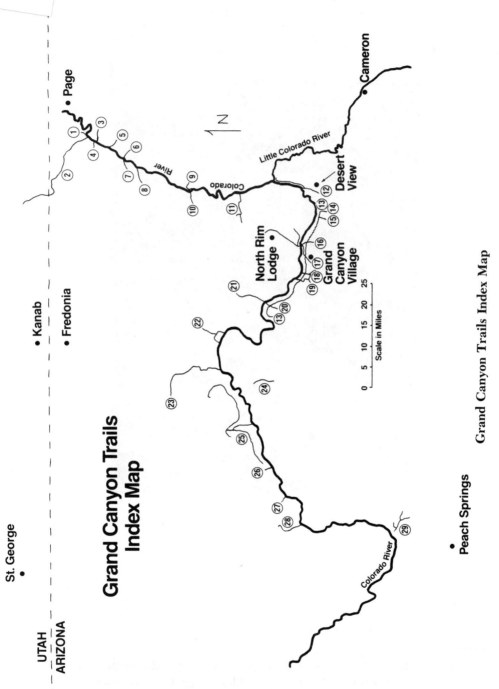

Grand Canyon Trails
Index Map

Grand Canyon Trails Index Map

Stewart Aitchison

# GRAND CANYON TRAIL #1

| | |
|---|---|
| Name: | Spencer Trail |
| Trail Location: | #1 on Index Map |
| Trailhead Elevation: | 3,180 feet |
| Total Vertical Ascent: | 1,500 feet |
| Length (one way): | About 1.5 miles |
| Maps: | U.S.G.S. Topos—Lee's Ferry; Grand Canyon Recreational Map #1 |
| Overall Difficulty: | Moderate; no water along route |
| Permit: | NPS; none required if done as a day hike |

The Lee's Ferry area is rich in western history. As early as 1776, Spanish padres were attempting to cross the Colorado River here. In 1871, the Mormon Church sent John D. Lee, one of the instigators of the infamous Mountain Meadow Massacre, to establish a ferry to allow missionaries and emigrants to travel from southern Utah into Arizona. Wagons slowly rolled their way along the base of the Vermilion Cliffs, were ferried across the then muddy Colorado, and out along Lee's Backbone, the rough rocky ramp leading to the Echo Cliffs. W.L. Rusho and C. Gregory Crampton have written an excellent history of this locale entitled *Desert River Crossing*.

The Spencer Trail begins 1/2 mile upstream from the end of Lee's Ferry parking lot. Follow the path that parallels the river. The Spencer Trail begins just about opposite the wreckage of the ship the *Charles H. Spencer*. The trail wastes no time in ascending the Vermilion Cliffs in a series of switchbacks thus giving the hiker superlative views of the Colorado River and the head of Marble Canyon, the beginning of the Grand Canyon.

This trail was built in 1910 by Charles Spencer, one of the more colorful prospectors and entrepreneurs to come to the Canyon country. He planned to transport coal from Warm Creek, some 28 miles to the north, to Lee's Ferry. The coal was going to be used in powering pumps and sluices to aid in his search for gold. After trail construction was completed, it was decided that the mule trains could not carry enough coal, so another more elaborate scheme was devised.

Spencer had a dismantled 92-foot-long paddle wheel steamboat hauled in by wagon and reconstructed at the mouth of Warm Creek.

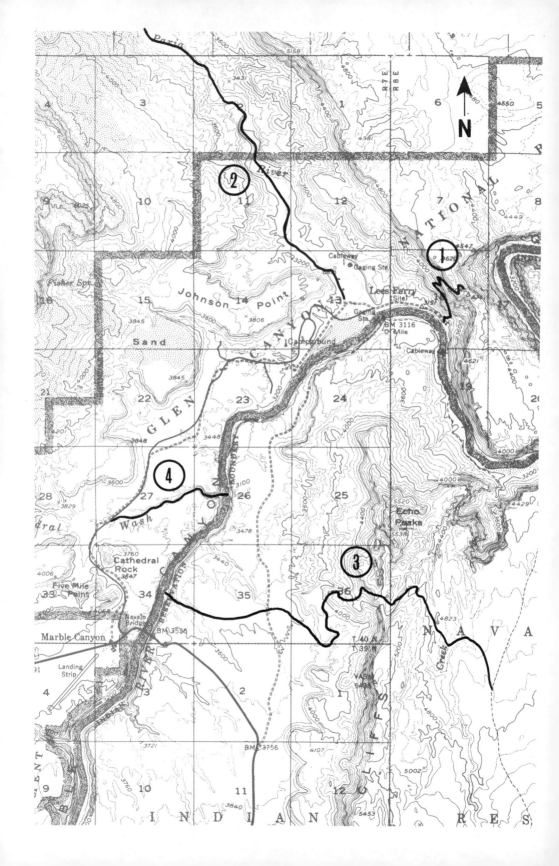

**The Ship** *Charles H. Spencer*

David Hubbard

The boat was christened the *Charles H. Spencer*, loaded up with coal, and set off for Lee's Ferry. Upon arrival at the Ferry, it was determined that all the coal the boat could carry would be needed just to make the round trip! By this time, though, tests showed that the amount of gold in the Chinle Shale at the base of the Vermilion Cliffs was too small to be profitable. The *Charles H. Spencer* was moored and eventually sank. For over 50 more years Charles Spencer prospected in the canyon area seeking his *El Dorado*.

The rocks of the Vermilion and Echo Cliffs overlie the Kaibab Limestone, which usually forms the rim of the Grand Canyon. The deep chocolate brown layers at the base of the cliffs belong to the Moenkopi Formation; above it is a pale-brown conglomerate called the Shinarump. Some uranium has been recovered from the Shinarump from the El Pequito Mine, 1 mile west of Lee's Ferry.

The blue-green shales above the Shinarump are the Chinle, a betoni-tic clay sometimes containing petrified wood. This is the same forma-tion that makes up the Painted Desert and Petrified Forest. Forming the vertical cliffs are the Moenave, Kayenta, and Navajo Formations. These three may be hard to distinguish because there are not always sharp lines of contact between each one.

The Moenave is reddish-brown in color. The Kayenta is lighter in color and sometimes strikingly cross-bedded. The buff-colored Navajo sandstone may erode into the arches and domes often seen along the top of the cliffs.

If you have a pair of binoculars along, it's often possible to see beaver swimming in the river and the dark bodies of huge trout that lurk in the cold water.

**Marble Canyon**

From John W. Powell, 1895; *Canyons of the Colorado*. Reprinted by Dover Publications, N.Y., 1961 under the title: *The Exploration of the Colorado River and Its Canyons*.

# GRAND CANYON TRAIL #2

Name:                        Paria Canyon
Trail Location:              #2 on the Index Map
Trailhead Elevation:         4,320 feet at White House Ruins
                             parking area
Total Vertical Descent:      About 1,200 feet to Lee's Ferry
Length (one way):            35 miles; plan 4 to 6 days
Maps:                        U.S.G.S. Topos—Paria, Paria
                             Plateau, Lee's Ferry; B.L.M.—Paria
                             Canyon Map
Overall Difficulty:          Moderate
Permit:                      Bureau of Land Management


The best way to hike Paria Canyon is to start from the Bureau of Land Management parking lot located at the old homestead site called White House Ruins. Just a little east of the Paria River Bridge on Highway 89 you will see the B.L.M. Ranger Station. You may obtain a hiking permit here during the summer only. During other seasons you must check in with the Kanab District Office, 320 North 1st East, Kanab, UT 84741, phone: (801) 644-2672. White House Ruins is 3 miles farther down the unpaved road leading from the ranger station. The B.L.M. gives out a map that contains a mile-by-mile description of points of interest.

Although it is possible to hike (run?) to Lee's Ferry in three days or less, four days should be considered the minimum time to enjoy the canyon. Since most of the walking involves wading, sturdy tennis shoes, army jungle boots, or other canvas boots are recommended.

The Paria River has sliced its way through the Navajo, Kayenta, and Moenave Sandstones to form one of the most beautiful slickrock canyons in northern Arizona. Fresh water seeps form lovely hanging gardens of maidenhair fern and columbines. A narrow side-canyon called Buckskin Gulch invites exploration where the canyon walls press together as close as 3 feet.

From a point 4.2 miles from the parking area to mile 9.0, Paria Canyon is also narrow and no really safe campsite exists. The monsoon season of July, August, and September makes the hike dangerous. The Paria and Buckskin drain a huge area and deadly flash floods can roar through the canyon.

Just such a flood in the fall of 1980 formed a deep, 100-yard-long pool near the confluence of the Paria with Buckskin. Supposedly it is deep enough that you must swim. Beware of hypothermia! More than one strong swimmer has drowned when underestimating the debilitating effect of cold water.

In dry years, there may be no water in the Paria River and some of the seeps and springs disappear. When flowing, the springs are potable but the river water should be purified.

Early Mormon ranchers attempted to pump river water 1,000 feet up to the dry Paria Plateau. Remains of their pumps and pipeline can be seen at mile 15.6.

A couple of miles farther, Wrather Canyon enters from the south. A half-mile up Wrather is a 200-foot natural arch, one of the largest in Arizona. Prehistoric Anasazi petroglyphs can be found here as well as in the main canyon.

From here to Lee's Ranch and cemetery (located 1 mile from Lee's Ferry), the main canyon widens out and a number of side canyons invite exploration. Take a few minutes to poke around Lee's Ranch and try to imagine what it must have been like to live in such an isolated spot . . . a place that Emma Lee (one of John D. Lee's many wives) called the "Lonely Dell."

# GRAND CANYON TRAIL #3

| | |
|---|---|
| Name: | CCC Trail |
| Trail Location: | #3 on the Index Map |
| Trailhead Elevation: | 3,520 feet where dirt crosses trail |
| Total Vertical Ascent: | About 1,300 feet to top of Echo Cliffs/descent to river is about 400 feet |
| Length (one way): | About 3.5 miles to top of Echo Cliffs; about 1.5 miles to river |
| Maps: | U.S.G.S. Topos—Lee's Ferry; Grand Canyon Recreational Map #1 |
| Overall Difficulty: | Easy to Moderate |
| Permit: | Navajo |

About 1.6 miles east of Navajo Bridge on Highway 89A you will find a dirt road heading north. There are actually several dirt roads, which is usually the case on the Navajo Indian Reservation. They all seem to come together, and in about 1 mile from the pavement the road drops into a wash. When the road climbs back out of the wash, pull off and park. Just about due east is where this trail begins its ascent of the Echo Cliffs. The trail shown on the Grand Canyon Recreation Map Series #1 is a good approximation of the route. As you begin to climb, you will encounter old roads and sheep trails. Trail construction is visible most of the way. The view from the crest is magnificent . . . the great gash of Marble Canyon in the foreground, the Vermilion Cliffs stretching away to the Kaibab Plateau.

An old Indian trail, the Buzzard Highline, takes off to the north about 1 mile east of the crest but is in such poor condition it is not recommended.

The Grand Canyon Recreational Map Series #1 shows the trail continuing from where you left your car, down the wash to the Colorado River. This is a pleasant walk but does *not* let you down to the river's edge. The trail actually goes down the unnamed wash about 1 mile south. Trail construction is visible switchbacking down to the river, but is so badly eroded that extreme care should be exercised following this route.

It's believed that this trail was built in the 1930's by the Civilian Conservation Corps to allow Navajos to bring sheep off the Kaibito Plateau down to the river.

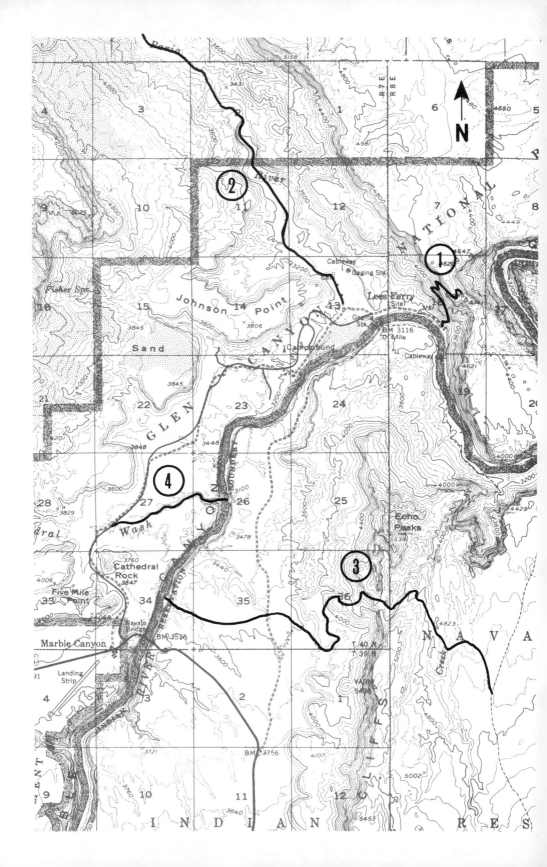

The Echo Peaks received their name from Frederick Dellenbaugh and two other members of John W. Powell's 1871 Colorado River expedition when they climbed the north summit of the three peaks. Dellenbaugh fired his Remington revolver. The loud report was followed by silence and then ". . . the peal after peal of the echoing shot came back . . ."

**View of Marble Canyon from Vermilion Cliffs**

From John W. Powell, 1895; *Canyons of the Colorado.* Reprinted by Dover Publications, N.Y., 1961 under the title: *The Exploration of the Colorado River and Its Canyons.*

# GRAND CANYON TRAIL #4

| | |
|---|---|
| Name: | Cathedral Wash |
| Trail Location: | #4 on Index Map |
| Trailhead Elevation: | 3,340 feet |
| Total Vertical Descent: | 340 feet |
| Length: | About 1.5 miles |
| Maps: | U.S.G.S. Topo—Lee's Ferry; Grand Canyon Recreational Map #1 |
| Overall Difficulty: | Easy |
| Permit: | NPS; none if done as a day hike |

Turn off Highway 89A onto the Lee's Ferry Road. Drive about 1.3 miles and you will see a pull-out on your left; park here. There is a park service interpretive sign located here about the local geology.

To begin the hike, walk to the wash immediately north of the parking area. Cathedral Wash takes its name from the chocolate-colored monolith, Cathedral Rock, on your right. Cathedral Rock is composed of Moenkopi shales capped by resistant Shinarump Conglomerate. These formations date from the Mesozoic Era and once covered the Kaibab Limestone, which forms the rim of the Grand Canyon. Erosion has removed most of these younger rocks except where they are protected by a harder cap-rock.

The walk to the river takes about an hour. You pass through a pretty "narrows" section and come out on a small, sandy beach.

# GRAND CANYON TRAIL #5

Name:                     Jackass Canyon
Trail Location:           #5 on the Index Map
Trailhead Elevation:      3,900 feet
Total Vertical Descent:   800 feet
Length (one way):         About 2.5 miles
Maps:                     U.S.G.S. Topos—Tanner Wash; Lee's
                          Ferry; Grand Canyon Recreational
                          Map #1
Overall Difficulty:       Easy to Moderate
Permit:                   Navajo

This route is accessible from Highway 89A. Park near milepost 532 which is about 2 miles south of Navajo Spring. At the highway there are several washes which quickly join to form a canyon. After about 1.5 miles, you join the main branch of Jackass and another mile brings you to the Colorado River within Marble Canyon.

Jackass Canyon is one of the easier routes to the river and has interesting "narrows." A fixed cable helps hikers descend one of several minor barrier falls. Gloves are helpful since the wire cable is frayed. (The cable has recently disappeared.)

It is possible to walk downstream along the bank of the Colorado to Salt Water Wash (Grand Canyon Trail #7) thus making a loop-trip back out to the highway.

Badger Creek Rapids at the mouth of Jackass are the first major rapids river-runners encounter after departing from Lee's Ferry. The rapids result from boulders being washed into the river by Badger Creek and Jackass during flash floods.

In Marble Canyon, it may be difficult to differentiate the Kaibab Limestone, Toroweap Formation and the Coconino Sandstone because they all tend to be cliff-forming and weathering has concealed sedimentary details. The Toroweap can be distinguished from the Kaibab by its thinner bedding and from the Coconino by its lack of large-scale crossbedding. Jackass Canyon is one of the best places to observe the three formations and their mutual contacts.

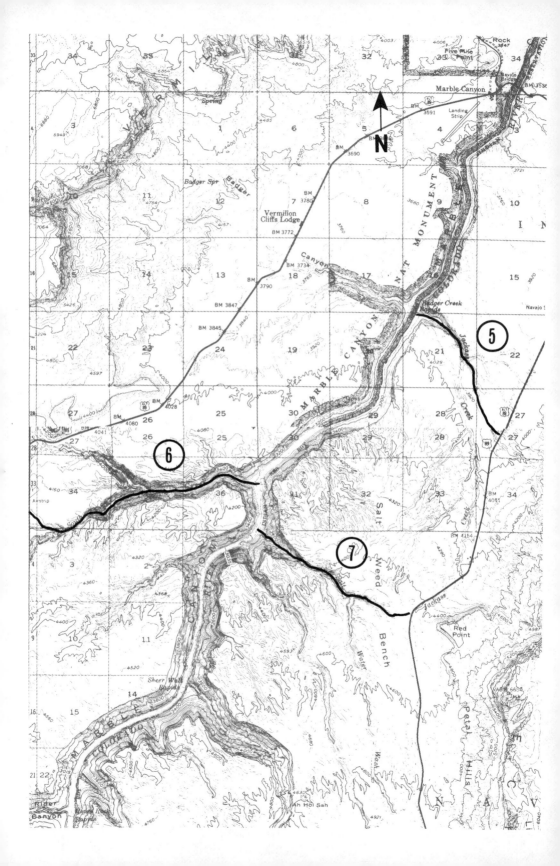

# GRAND CANYON TRAIL #6

| | |
|---|---|
| Name: | Soap Creek |
| Trail Location: | #6 on the Index Map |
| Trailhead Elevation: | 4,200 feet |
| Total Vertical Descent: | About 1,200 feet |
| Length (one way): | About 4.5 miles |
| Maps: | U.S.G.S. Topos—Emmett Wash; Tanner Wash; Grand Canyon Recreational Map #1 |
| Overall Difficulty: | Moderate; some scrambling |
| Permit: | NPS |

This is another route accessible from Highway 89A. About 1 mile south of the Cliff Dweller's Lodge, there is a small airstrip on the east side of the highway. A small canyon leads from the airstrip into the South Fork of Soap Creek Canyon. (The North Fork is for climbers only.)

Some scrambling is required and in certain sections the canyon floor is littered with large boulders. Expect to take about three hours, one-way, to reach the river.

Soap Creek and Badger Creek, upstream, supposedly received their names from an incident involving the Mormon missionary Jacob Hamblin. Hamblin killed a badger on the wash that bears its name. He carried the animal to the next creek south and then put the badger in a kettle to boil. By the following morning the alkali in the water had combined with the animal fat to form soap.

Soap Creek Rapids are the second set of major rapids encountered by boatmen coming from Lee's Ferry. The rapids are formed by boulders washing into the river from Soap Creek and also talus blocks from the east wall falling into the river. The vivid red Hermit Shale is exposed at river level across from the mouth of Soap Creek.

In the spring of 1872, several prospectors stole much of the equipment that had been cached at Lee's Ferry for the second Powell expedition, and started downstream on rafts. They made it through Badger Creek Rapids but wrecked at Soap Creek. They lost all of their possessions. They escaped out of the Canyon by going up Soap Creek, presumably the North Fork, since they had to make driftwood ladders and use clothes as ropes.

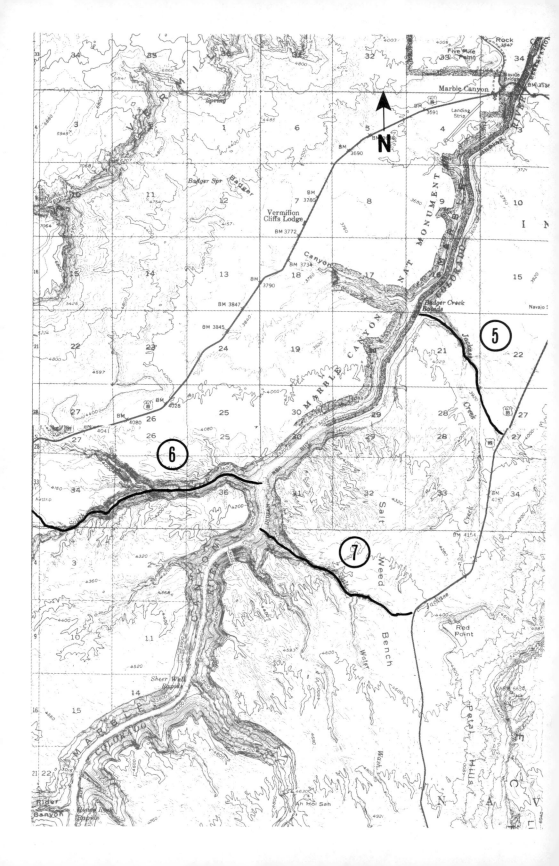

# GRAND CANYON TRAIL #7

| | |
|---|---|
| Name: | Salt Water Wash |
| Trail Location: | #7 on the Index Map |
| Trailhead Elevation: | 4,500 feet |
| Total Vertical Descent: | 1,500 feet |
| Length (one way): | About 3 miles |
| Maps: | U.S.G.S. Topo—Tanner Wash; Grand Canyon Recreational Map #1 |
| Overall Difficulty: | Moderate |
| Permit: | Navajo |

Salt Water Wash can be reached by starting down a drainage at about milepost 529 on Highway 89A. Consult the Tanner Wash topo to make sure you do not start down the upper part of Jackass Canyon by mistake. There are some signs of trail construction but for the most part just follow the bed of the wash. As you approach the mouth of the Canyon, be careful descending the loose talus.

Although the major rapid Soap Creek is located less than a mile upstream, it was in the rather mild-looking water near the mouth of Salt Water Wash that Frank M. Brown drowned on July 10, 1889. Brown had recently organized the Denver, Colorado Canyon, and Pacific Railroad Company for the purpose of surveying a possible Colorado to San Diego railroad through the Canyon. A member of the party, Peter Hansbrough, carved an inscription about Brown's death. This inscription can still be seen. It is near river level a short distance below the mouth of Salt Water Wash and faces downstream.

Five days after Brown's death. Hansbrough and Henry Richards were drowned, and the remainder of the party abandoned the river. They climbed out of Marble Canyon by going up South Canyon (Grand Canyon Trail #10). The survey was completed the following year under the direction of engineer Robert B. Stanton, a member of the original group. Although Stanton's survey convinced him that the railroad was feasible, monetary backers for the project did not materialize.

**Brown Inscription**

David Hubbard

# GRAND CANYON TRAIL #8

| | |
|---|---|
| Name: | Rider Canyon |
| Trail Location: | #8 on the Index Map |
| Trailhead Elevation: | 4,500 feet |
| Total Vertical Descent: | 1,500 feet |
| Length (one way): | About 4 miles |
| Maps: | U.S.G.S. Topos—Emmett Wash, Tanner Wash; Grand Canyon Recreational Map #1, Trailhead incorrectly shown. |
| Overall Difficulty: | Difficult, very steep at beginning |
| Permit: | NPS |

To reach the trailhead, drive about .25 miles west of milepost 557 on Highway 89A. (This is about 10 miles southwest of Cliff Dweller's Lodge.) Turn south onto a dirt road and pass through the gate. Please leave all gates as you find them.

Now carefully watch your odometer:

At   .3—Take the left fork

     1.7—Take the left fork

     2.2—Pass over a cattle guard

     2.3—Take the left fork

     3.5—Pass through a gate

     4.3—Cross House Rock Wash

     4.9—Arrive at Kram (also spelled Cram) Ranch

Take the road around the west side of the ranch buildings heading south.

     5.5—Pass through fence

     5.8—Take the left fork

     6.8—Pass through fence

The road begins to deteriorate and may be difficult for a low-slung car.

     9.2—Take the right fork

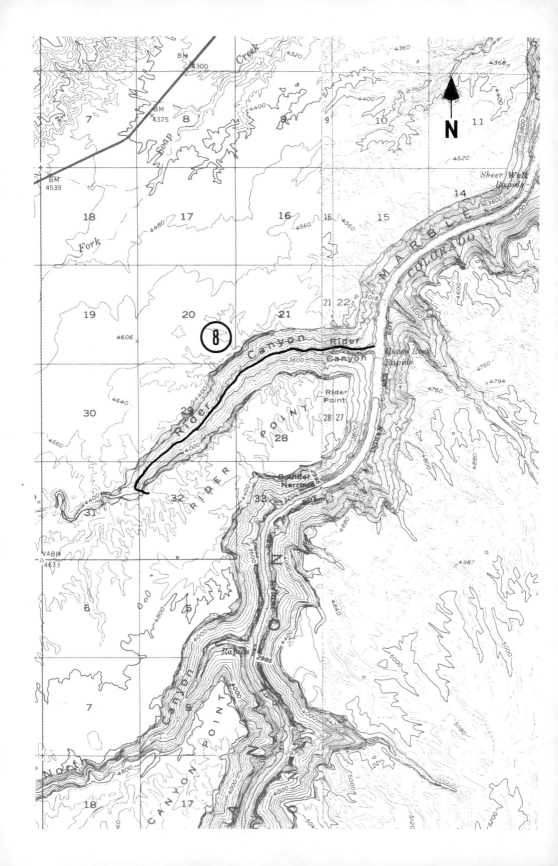

12.3—At intersection in the bottom of a drainage, go right or downstream

12.8—The road abruptly ends on the very edge of Marble Canyon overlooking the Colorado River in the vicinity of Boulder Narrows. Plan about 1.5 hours to drive from the pavement to this point.

Walk NNW about 1 mile to intersect the south rim of Rider Canyon. Just about due south of the letter "d" in Rider on the Emmett Wash topo, the rim is broken by several long fractures (joints) parallel to the canyon.

One of these breaks is marked by rock cairns. Descending this fracture through the Kaibab Limestone, you will encounter two places where it is necessary to crawl under chockstones. Then you are on a steep and loose talus slope. Watch your step!

A faint trail drops practically straight down the slope to the floor of Rider Canyon. From here to the Colorado River, the route is mainly along the canyon bottom. At one point, a 30-foot drop necessitates climbing *up* to the left (north) and then down.

The name of the canyon is a corruption of Ryder. Ryder was a cowboy whom the members of the 1909 Stone River expedition had met at Lee's Ferry.

In late December, 1889, Robert Stanton was leading a river expedition down the Colorado to determine whether or not a railroad could be built through the Grand Canyon. Not far from Rider Canyon, F.A. Nims, the expedition's photographer, fell 20 feet while trying to take a picture. His leg was fractured. They splinted the poor fellow's leg as best they could and decided to try to carry him out to the rim via Rider Canyon. Stanton found the route out and walked all the way to Lee's Ferry to fetch a wagon and help. Stanton took over as photographer, with no previous experience, and managed to expose 2,200 negatives during the rest of the river journey.

There are many interesting fossils to be seen in the limestone boulders along the bottom of Rider Canyon. Brachiopods and crinoids have been replaced with the mineral chert and are exposed as orange and black fossil casts.

Seep willow, rabbitbrush, prince's plume, prickly pear, and pale hoptree are some of the plants growing in Rider. Barrel cactus begins to appear near the Colorado.

Look for blue-green collared lizards sunning on top of large boulders and chuckwallas, the canyon's largest lizard, up to 16 inches long, in crevices. Red-spotted toads may be breeding in rain pools.

The descending notes of the Canyon wren's song are frequently heard along with the buzz of rock wrens.

At the mouth of Rider Canyon is one of the Colorado's best rapids, House Rock. The name is derived from one of the upper drainages into Rider where early travelers used to camp and someone inscribed on a rock the words, "Rock House Hotel."

# GRAND CANYON TRAIL #9

| | |
|---|---|
| Name: | Shinumo Wash (Twenty-Nine Mile Canyon) |
| Trail Location: | #9 on the Index Map |
| Trailhead Elevation: | 5,400 feet |
| Total Vertical Descent: | 3,500 feet |
| Length (one way): | About 3 to 5 hours from rim to river |
| Maps: | U.S.G.S. Topos—Emmett Wash; Nankoweap |
| Overall Difficulty: | Moderate to Difficult |
| Permit: | Navajo and NPS |

Driving on the Navajo Indian Reservation is always challenging. Roads lead everywhere and nowhere. One approach to this trail is to start at the Cedar Ridge. Trading Post on Highway 89. Drive west from the trading post staying on what appears to be the most used dirt road. About 7 miles from the highway the road forks. The one to the right (northwest) should head toward the large, flat-topped mesa, Shinumo Altar, in the distance. About 5.5 more miles and you should be passing the southern flank of Shinumo Altar.

Continue heading more or less northwesterly another 10 miles to the rim of Marble Canyon. About 1.5 miles back from the angle formed by the Marble Canyon rim and the Shinumo Wash rim, there is a cairn marking the trailhead.

One story says that cattle thieves originally built this trail to hide their stolen stock in Shinumo Wash. The Bureau of Reclamation improved the trail during the 1940's to allow them to take horses to the river. It was at this location that a major dam on the Colorado was proposed. During the early 1920's, the U.S. Geological Survey mapped the Colorado River and its major tributaries and examined a number of potential dam sites. If this dam had been built, a reservoir would have inundated the river and riparian habitat almost all the way back to Lee's Ferry, some 30 river miles upstream. Fortunately Marble Canyon was included in Grand Canyon National Park in 1975 and hopefully this will prevent a dam from ever being constructed.

The trail quickly descends through the Kaibab, Toroweap, and Coconino Formations to the bed of Shinumo Wash. Parts of the trail

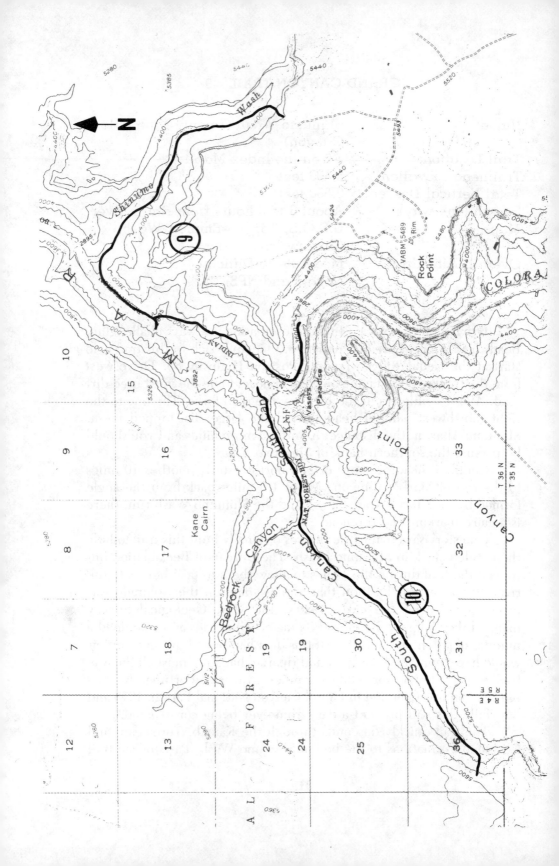

can be followed along the left (south) slope which is probably faster than boulder-hopping down the wash bottom. Upon reaching the top of the Redwall Limestone, the trail veers left. Progress directly down the wash is impossible without ropes. About 1.5 miles below Shinumo Wash the trail forks. The right fork goes down to the river's edge and some warm springs. The left fork continues on top of the Redwall for about another 4 miles, ending a little upstream from Redwall Cavern. *However*, to get off the Redwall and to the river requires climbing experience and possibly a rope.

On the opposite cliff about 3 miles from Shinumo is Vasey's Paradise, a delightful spring gushing out of a cave in the Redwall. Powell named this spot after a botanist friend, George W. Vasey. During the spring and summer, yellow and crimson monkeyflowers and watercress abound.

Just upstream from Vasey's, also on the opposite wall, is Stanton's Cave. It was here that split-twig figurines were discovered that radio-carbon-dated at 3,000 to 4,000 years old. (See Grand Canyon Trail #10.)

A couple of years ago I was on a raft trip and we came upon two very cold and frightened hikers stranded on the gravel island in front of Vasey's. These fellows had hiked down the Shinumo Trail, rappelled down the Redwall, and attempted to swim across the river. The frigid water and powerful currents exhausted them and they had barely reached the island. They were shivering and considering swimming back to shore, the first a symptom of hypothermia; the second a sign of stupidity. Do *not* swim in the Colorado! We gave them a ride to shore.

### The Heart of Marble Canyon

From John W. Powell, 1895; *Canyons of the Colorado*. Reprinted by
Dover Publications, N.Y., 1961 under the title: *The Exploration of the
Colorado River and Its Canyons.*

# GRAND CANYON TRAIL #10

| | |
|---|---|
| Name: | South Canyon |
| Trail Location: | #10 on the Index Map |
| Trailhead Elevation: | 5,600 feet |
| Total Vertical Descent: | 2,725 feet |
| Length (one way): | About 6 miles |
| Maps: | U.S.G.S. Topos—Nankoweap, Emmett Wash |
| Overall Difficulty: | Very difficult; previous canyon hiking experience recommended |
| Permit: | NPS |

This route allows access to Vasey's Paradise, Stanton's Cave, and other interesting features in the heart of Marble Canyon. Route is the best term for this way into the Canyon; a trail it is not.

See Grand Canyon Trail #11 for driving directions to the House Rock Valley Buffalo Ranch. At the ranch you may ask for directions to the rim of South Canyon. A dirt track takes you near the head of the Canyon. There is an old trash dump here containing hundreds of muledeer antlers. Note where a fence meets the rim. About 150 feet west of this point a crack in the Kaibab Limestone permits a descent to the talus slope below. In the limestone keep an eye open for brachiopod fossils stained red with iron oxides. In the Coconino Sandstone are numerous fossilized reptile or amphibian tracks.

Follow the floor of South Canyon toward the Colorado until you are on top of the Redwall Limestone and near the mouth of the Canyon. Contour on top of the Redwall to the north (upriver) and there is a faint trail leading through the limestone to the river's edge.

There are other ways off of the north rim of South Canyon including at least two routes through Bedrock Canyon. All require careful route-finding, a good sense of balance, and cautionary discretion.

It was in 1889 that Robert Stanton and the remaining part of the ill-fated Brown Expedition (see Grand Canyon Trail #7) escaped from Marble Canyon by climbing out South Canyon. But they certainly were not the first to visit this area.

In the large cave (now called Stanton's Cave), just downstream

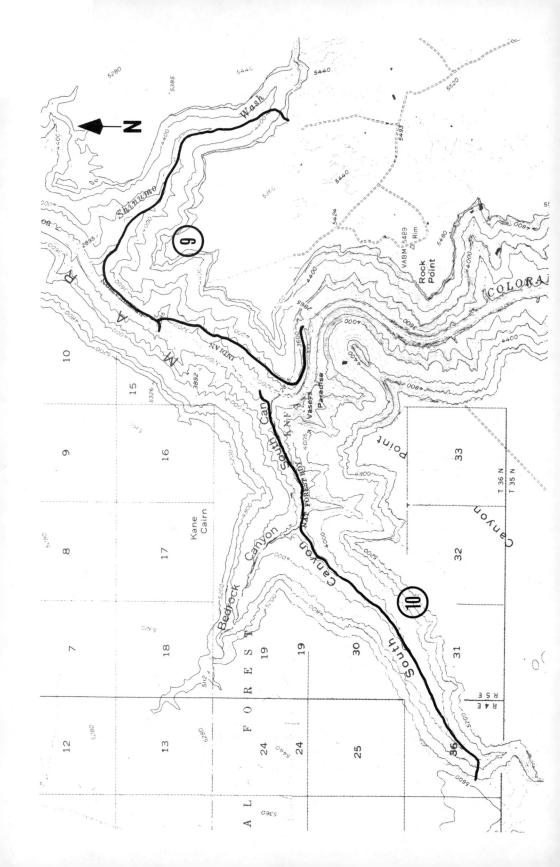

from the mouth of South Canyon, have been found figurines made of split-willow twigs. Radio-carbon-dating shows that these are 3,000 to 4,000 years old. They were placed in the cave by an enigmatic people called the Pinto Basin-Desert Culture, a group of hunters and gatherers of wild plants who roamed the Southwest 25,000 to 8,000 years ago.

Also discovered in Stanton's Cave have been the bones of giant condors, saber-toothed tigers, and other animals that have been extinct in North America for at least 10,000 years. Please do not enter the cave since further scientific information can be gathered only if the cave floor is undisturbed.

And speaking of bones, you may have noticed a human skeleton near the mouth of South Canyon. No one knows who this hapless person was; perhaps an Indian or a prospector. The skeleton minus skull was first discovered by the Swain-Hatch river party of 1934. Since then souvenir collectors have ravaged these poor fellow's bones. Please do not desecrate this site any further.

Downstream from Stanton's Cave is the verdant Vasey's Paradise, a beautiful spring gushing out of the Redwall Limestone cliff. Geologist-explorer John Wesley Powell named this garden after his friend George Vasey, who was a botanist and had accompanied Powell on some overland trips in the West. Spelunkers have climbed into the dry cave next to the spring and have explored over 2 miles of passageways.

Plants growing at Vasey's include red and yellow monkeyflower, maidenhair fern, watercress, horsetails, common reed, redbud trees, Apache plume, willow, Rocky Mountain beeplant, paintbrush, and milkweed. Watch out for the poison ivy, too.

Farther downstream and on the opposite side of the Colorado, you can see huge Redwall Cavern. Powell estimated that 50,000 people could be seated inside. Although not quite that large, the cavern is nonetheless an impressive cut into the Redwall Limestone.

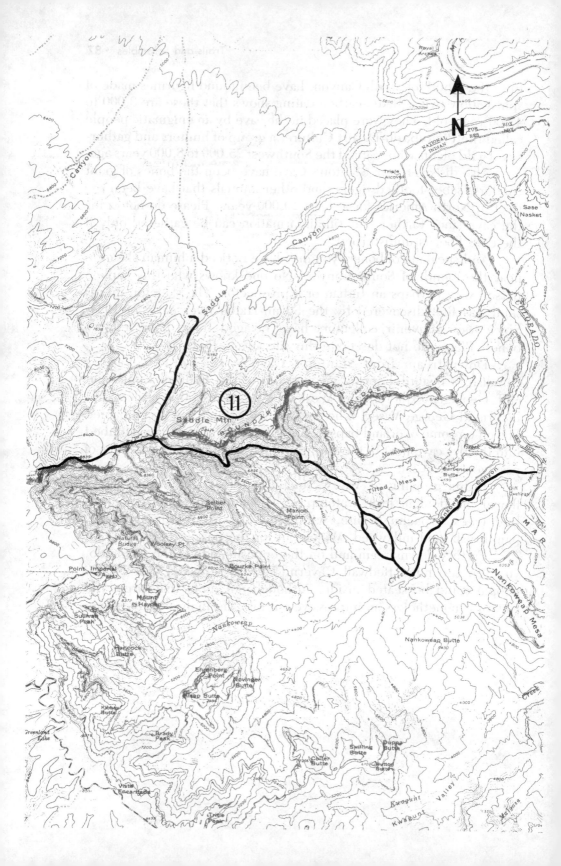

# GRAND CANYON TRAIL #11

| | |
|---|---|
| Name: | Nankoweap |
| Trail Location: | #11 on the Index Map |
| Trailhead Elevation: | 7,600 feet at Saddle Mountain Saddle |
| Total Vertical Descent: | About 4,800 feet |
| Length (one way): | About 14 miles from Saddle Mountain Saddle to the Colorado River |
| Maps: | U.S.G.S. Topos—Nankoweap |
| Overall Difficulty: | Difficult, virtually no shade; no water until you reach Nankoweap Creek. Plan minimum of three days for round trip to river and back. |
| Permit: | NPS |

There are two approaches to this trailhead. One is from Forest Service Road #610 which takes off from Highway 67 about 1.5 miles north of the North Rim Entrance Station to the park. Follow #610 to its end; a rock cairn marks the trail. Note two hills to the east. The trail first descends to a saddle, then passes north of the first hill, and then to a saddle between the two hills. Continue around the south slope of the second hill and you will come to a relatively flat area. Cross the flat northeasterly but do not go into a drainage leading off to the north. At the far end of the flat, the trail turns more to the east and drops into the saddle immediately west of Saddle Mountain. At this point the Nankoweap Trail begins its descent into the Canyon.

The other approach to Saddle Mountain is to take the House Rock Buffalo Ranch Road south from Highway 89A. The turnoff is approximately 20 miles east of Jacob Lake. Go past the Buffalo Ranch turnoff to the end of Forest Service Road #445 G. An advantage to this approach is that the road is open most of the winter; whereas, the North Rim highway is usually closed from mid-November through mid-May. Also you are likely to see mule deer, pronghorn antelope, and, of course, buffalo as you drive to Saddle Mountain.

At the end of Forest Service Road #445 G look for a rock cairn on the northeast side of the parking area. This marks the trail to Saddle Mountain. The trail first descends into a small canyon, follows the bottom, and then climbs up a slope toward the saddle. The trail is vague but just keep aiming for the obvious saddle to the south.

Either approach to this saddle takes over an hour.

From the saddle the Nankoweap Trail switchbacks down through the red Hermit Shale and levels off about 100 feet below the top of the Supai. Cliffrose, manzanita, and buffalo-berry crowd the slim trail.

The trail then contours east and south all the way to a saddle west of Tilted Mesa. The trail is badly eroded through the Redwall Limestone but is usually marked with cairns. After switchbacking through the Redwall, the trail goes left of a knob of rock. About 1 mile past the knob, scramble down a rockslide (watch your footing) toward an outcrop of pink rock. Continue over the outcrop, down the slope composed of Bright Angel Shale, and eventually to a steep drainage leading down into Nankoweap Creek. Either follow the drainage or traverse left through the shale to the Tapeats Sandstone where the old trail again reappears. You can reach the Colorado by following Nankoweap Creek. There is usually water in Nankoweap Creek.

The upper drainages leading into the Nankoweap basin are also worth visiting. In the branch north of Woolsey Point, a perennial spring feeds a delightful waterfall. The drainage between Woolsey and Mt. Hayden contains the largest natural bridge in the Grand Canyon. Senator Barry Goldwater discovered it from the air a number of years ago.

The ancient Anasazi occupied the Nankoweap basin as demonstrated by the many fine ruins scattered about. Please remember that the ruins and artifacts are protected by law. Please do not disturb them. One particularly impressive cliff dwelling is located high in the Redwall facing the Colorado River just south of the mouth of Nankoweap. (I have just learned that vandals pushed over some of the walls during 1983.) The terraces above the river were once planted with small plots of maize, beans, and squash. Today native plants like prickly pear cactus, blackbrush, and mesquite have reclaimed the land.

Later Paiutes roamed the Nankoweap area. Supposedly the Paiute name Nankoweap refers to an Indian battle that took place near Saddle Mountain.

In 1882, John Wesley Powell, then director of the U.S. Geological Survey, supervised the construction of a horse trail into Nankoweap Canyon so that geologist Charles Walcott could study the Precambrian rocks.

Several years later, horse thieves began to utilize this route. They would steal horses in Utah, drive them down the Nankoweap Trail, ride along the river or follow the fault running west of Nankoweap Mesa, Kwagunt Butte, and Chuar Butte, ford the Colorado, and go out the Tanner Trail. The horses were then sold to unsuspecting customers in the Flagstaff area. The thieves would then steal horses in Arizona and reverse the operation.

During the Prohibition Era of the 1920's illegal moonshine was transported along this route. As recently as 1937, horses were used on this trail but one was lost over a cliff. Today it is hard to imagine the Nankoweap Trail ever being good enough for horse travel.

This is the best area to see the younger Precambrian rocks, those that once formed block-faulted mountains. There is also a striking example of more recent faulting. The East Kaibab Fault runs along the western base of Nankoweap Mesa, Kwagunt Butte, Chuar Butte, and Temple Butte. The rock layers east of the fault are 1,000 or more feet lower than the corresponding layers west of the fault. For example look west to the Kaibab Plateau. The Kaibab Limestone forming the rim is 8,000 or more feet above sea level. Now look east to the far rim of Marble Canyon; the Kaibab Limestone is about 6,000 feet above sea level. Look at the strata along the fault proper and you will notice that they are twisted and upturned, even vertical in places.

The biology of the Nankoweap Basin is equally as interesting. Along the Colorado are large sandy beaches. Adjacent to the river grow salt cedar (tamarisk), seepwillow, coyote willow, and arrowweed. Along the pre-Glen Canyon Dam highwater line can be found mesquite, catclaw, prince's plume, red brome, and pepper grass. Where the trail first hits Nankoweap Creek, there is a small oasis of Fremont cottonwood trees. In the upper drainages of Nankoweap are small stands of ponderosa pine, white fir, and Douglas fir.

Mule deer and coyotes inhabit the Nankoweap basin along with rock wrens, canyon wrens, pinyon jays, house finches, and sparrow hawks. Sometimes birds more typical of the Kaibab Plateau will venture into the lower canyon such as Steller's jays, Clark's nutcrackers, and hairy woodpeckers.

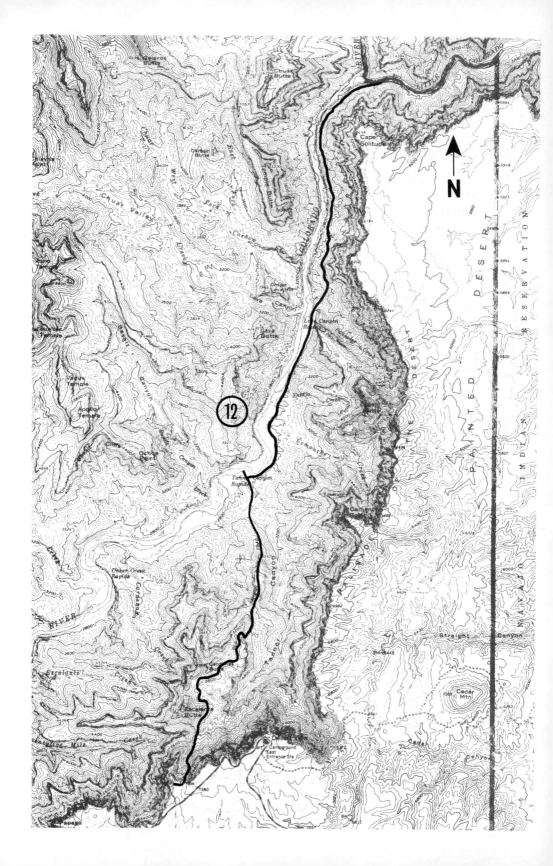

# GRAND CANYON TRAIL #12

| | |
|---|---|
| Name: | Tanner Trail (and Beamer Trail) |
| Trail Location: | #12 on the Index Map |
| Trailhead Elevation: | 7,300 feet |
| Total Vertical Descent: | 4,700 feet to Colorado River |
| Length (one way): | About 9 miles to Colorado River; about 4 miles from Tanner Rapids to Palisades Creek; about 5 miles from Palisades Creek to Little Colorado River. |
| Maps: | U.S.G.S. Topo—Vishnu Temple; Grand Canyon Recreation Map #3 |
| Overall Difficulty: | Moderate, hot and dry; no water until reaching Colorado River |
| Permit: | NPS |

Near Lipan Point, just a couple of miles west of Desert View on the East Rim Drive, the Tanner Trail descends into one of the most open areas of the Canyon. Superb Canyon vistas are seen to the north and the west. The Painted Desert shimmers off to the east.

Leave your car in the Lipan Point parking lot and walk back down (south) the road a hundred feet or so, turn east, go through the pinyon-juniper woodland a hundred yards to the head of a drainage leading north into the canyon. A sign marks the trail. The trail drops steadily in a series of switchbacks through the Kaibab, Toroweap, and Coconino formations before leveling off just south of Escalante Butte. The Tanner then contours around Escalante and Cardenas Buttes slowly descending through the Hermit and Supai formations. Steep switchbacks take you through the Redwall and then the trail turns toward the Colorado River and angles downward but staying parallel to Tanner Canyon. Not until the last half-mile does the trail drop into the bottom of Tanner Canyon.

The Tanner Trail receives enough use that route finding should be no problem for experienced hikers. It hasn't always been such. Back in 1959, a man and two boys lost their way. The man fell to his death while attempting to climb down a cliff. The boys found another way to the river but one of them died of thirst before reaching the

**Colorado River Scene**

From John W. Powell, 1895; *Canyons of the Colorado*. Reprinted by
Dover Publications, N.Y., 1961 under the title: *The Exploration of the
Colorado River and Its Canyons.*

water. (Some hikers, today, cache water along the trail for the trip out.) The lone survivor decided to try to float down the river to Phantom Ranch by hanging on to a driftwood log; a nearly fatal mistake. He made it to shore above Hance Rapids and tried walking back upstream. He was finally rescued by a park service helicopter.

The Anasazi and later the Hopi descended this route with some variations to reach homes within the Canyon and a sacred salt deposit near the mouth of the Little Colorado. It was near Lipan Point that the first Europeans saw the Grand Canyon. The Hopis led Garcia Lopez de Cardenas here in 1540, but did not disclose to the Spaniards that they knew of a way into the Canyon.

During the 1880's, Seth Tanner, A Mormon settler from Tuba City, prospected in eastern Grand Canyon. He used this old Indian trail and discovered a little copper and silver near the river. Remains of an old cabin and mine tunnels can be seen in the Palisades Creek area. Tanner improved the route and in 1889 with Fred Bunker and Lewis Bedlias relocated the upper trail to its present location.

As mentioned in the Nankoweap Trail description, this route became a favored trail for horse thieves. At the turn of the century, travel writer George James was descending the Tanner Trail and left his horses unattended farther up the trail. Several suspicious men passed James heading toward the rim. Later James discovered that his stock had been stolen.

In today's world, the hiker does not have to worry about horse thieves but car thefts are becoming a problem along the South Rim. Some things never change.

A trail leads from the mouth of Tanner Canyon upriver to the Little Colorado. Again this is an old Indian route which was upgraded by prospectors. For a time a prospector by the name of Ben Beamer took up residence in an Anasazi cliff dwelling a short distance up the Little Colorado River. He remodeled the door making it taller and added a window.

The Beamer Trail from Tanner to Palisades Creek is fairly distinct and is never far from the river's edge. At Palisades Creek the trail ascends a talus slope to the top of the Tapeats Sandstone where it contours all the way to the Little Colorado. It is a long day between Tanner and the Little Colorado with no water after leaving Palisades Creek and ascending to the top of the Tapeats.

Along this stretch of the Colorado are well-developed riparian habitats of salt cedar, seep-willow, coyote willow, and arrowweed. A couple of miles downstream from the Tanner Trail at Cardenas Creek is a small marsh complete with cattails, willows, beaver, and leopard frogs.

Among the native fish in the river are the Colorado River squawfish, the bonetail chub, and the humpback chub. They are adapted to swift, turbid waters and are either bottom feeders or prey on smaller fish. Since Glen Canyon Dam has changed the Colorado from the river "too thick to drink and too thin to plow" to a clear, cold river, the native fish have suffered. They are now mainly limited in distribution to the mouths of the major side streams such as the Little Colorado River, especially while breeding. Because of the importance of this area to the native fishery, no camping is allowed within 1 mile of the confluence of the Colorado and Little Colorado Rivers.

**Beamer's Cabin**

David Hubbard

**At the Mouth of the Little Colorado**

From John W. Powell, 1895; *Canyons of the Colorado*. Reprinted by
Dover Publications, N.Y., 1961 under the title: *The Exploration of the
Colorado River and Its Canyons*.

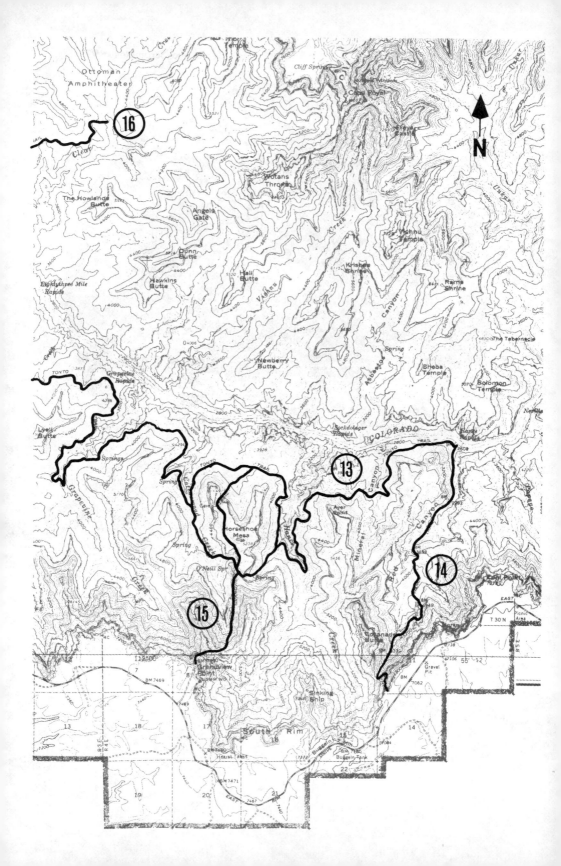

# GRAND CANYON TRAIL #13

Name:                      Tonto Trail
Trail Location:              #13 on the Index Map
Trailhead Elevation:        Averages about 3,000 feet
Total Vertical Descent:      ———
Length (one way):          Approximately 92 miles from Red
                                   Canyon to Garnet Canyon
Maps:                      U.S.G.S. Topos— Vishnu, Bright
                                   Angel, Havasupai Point; Grand
                                   Canyon Recreational Maps #3, 4, 5
Overall Difficulty:          Moderate to difficult, hot and dry
Permit:                    NPS

The Tonto Trail is normally used to connect two of the rim-to-river trails coming off the South Rim. This trail runs along the Tonto Plateau from Red Canyon (see Grand Canyon Trail #14) on the east to Garnet Canyon (see Grand Canyon Trail #20) on the west.

Mileages between trails are:

| | |
|---|---|
| Red Canyon (Hance Trail) to Cottonwood Creek (Grandview Trail): | 10 miles |
| Cotton Creek to South Kaibab: | 20 miles |
| South Kaibab to Bright Angel: | 5 miles |
| Bright Angel to Hermit: | 12 miles |
| Hermit to Boucher: | 8 miles |
| Boucher to Bass: | 22 miles |
| Bass to Garnet Canyon: | 15 miles |
| Total | 92 miles |

*Note:* There is no trail out of Garnet to the rim except via the Bass Trail.

Water is available in Hance, Pipe, Monument, Hermit, Boucher, and at Indian Gardens. Water may be found seasonally in Garnet, Ruby, Turquoise, Slate, Salt, Horn, Boulder, Grapevine, Lonetree, and Cottonwood. Other springs shown on the maps are either dry or undependable. Cottonwood Spring may be difficult to find. Getting off the Tonto Plateau down to the Colorado is rarely practical except at a few locations such as Garnet, Serpentine, Sapphire, Boucher, Hermit, and Monument, so do not count on drinking from the river.

The Tonto Trail is not nearly as level as it appears from the rim. Additionally the route is confused by numerous game and feral burro tracks. The best way to stay on the correct trail is to constantly scan ahead and try to pick out the most distinct trail on distant hills. Check the map frequently.

Because of the heavy use of the Tonto between Hermit and Indian Gardens, pit toilets and designated campsites have been set up at Horn, Salt, Monument, and Hermit. Please use them.

The Tonto Trail is hot and dry and sometimes frustrating as you contour endlessly in and out of every little wash and drainage. It has been said that for every 3 miles of contouring, you progress only 1 mile in a straight line—but what magnificent vistas and often exciting views into the Inner Gorge where the Colorado River is hemmed in by vertical walls of black schist.

The trail follows the top of the broad Tonto Plateau. Usually the trail is traversing over greenish Bright Angel Shale or brown Tapeats Sandstone. Occasionally it dips into the Precambrian rocks.

The vegetation is typical of the Great Basin Desert, endless stands of blackbrush, Mormon tea, snakeweed, prickly pear cactus, and an occasional Utah agave or banana yucca. Where permanent water exists, there are usually Fremont cottonwood trees along with other water-loving plants.

Canyon mice can be quite numerous at certain favorite campsites along the Tonto. I usually sleep with my pack nearby so that I can shoo them away during the night. The only problem with this idea is that once-in-a-while a desert spotted skunk is the nighttime camp raider. If you can lie still and do not scare the little beast, you will probably be spared a shower of horrible musk.

The Tonto is one of my favorite winter hikes but should be avoided during the heat of summer. Only idiots would try it then; perhaps that is how it received its name since Tonto (with apologies to the Lone Ranger's sidekick) is Spanish for foolish or silly.

**Niches or Panels in the Redwall Limestone (Over 600 Feet High)**

From John W. Powell, 1895, *Canyons of the Colorado*. Reprinted by Dover Publications, N.Y., 1961 under the title: *The Exploration of the Colorado River and Its Canyons*.

# GRAND CANYON TRAIL #14

| | |
|---|---|
| Name: | New Hance (Red Canyon) Trail |
| Trail Location: | #14 on the Index Map |
| Trailhead Elevation: | 7,000 feet |
| Total Vertical Descent: | 5,000 feet |
| Length (one way): | 8 miles |
| Maps: | U.S.G.S. Topos—Grandview Point, Vishnu Temple, Grand Canyon Recreation Map #4 |
| Overall Difficulty: | Very steep, hard to follow, no water until reaching Colorado River |
| Permit: | NPS |

Park your vehicle at Moran Point on the East Rim Drive. Walk about 1 mile southwest along the road until you come to a shallow drainage. Follow the drainage northwest about .25 mile to the rim. The trail is marked by a rock cairn. Allow at least six hours to descend and eight or more to hike back out.

This trail is receiving more use and cairns mark most of the route; but it is still very steep and in places obscure. The trail switchbacks steeply off the rim and passes through the Kaibab, Toroweap, and Coconino formations. Near the base of the Coconino, the route veers west into the drainage coming off the saddle south of Coronado Butte. Follow the drainage down through the Hermit and Supai to the top of the Redwall. The descent through the Redwall may be hard to find but it is marked by cairns and old lettering painted on the side of a rock. After the trail crosses a major drainage coming in from below Moran Point, it gently slopes downward into the bed of Red Canyon. Take note of this location. Some hikers have become lost on the return trip when they could not find the ascent out of Red Canyon. Follow the floor of Red Canyon to the Colorado River.

From the foot of New Hance you can go via the Tonto Trail westward to the Grandview Trail and beyond.

In the 1880's prospector John Hance came to the South Rim. He soon found that there was more gold in the pockets of tourists than the walls of the Grand Canyon. He built a hotel at the head of Hance Canyon and a trail down the east arm of Hance Canyon. This route is usually referred to as the Old Hance Trail. Rock slides in 1894 destroyed the upper half of the trail so Hance built a new one down Red Canyon.

Hance was one of the Canyon's best storytellers. A favorite tale was about the time the Canyon was socked-in with clouds and Hance decided to snowshoe across. He nearly died when the Canyon suddenly cleared and he was stranded on a pinnacle. But even with all of his imaginative wit, Hance was stumped one day for an answer when upon telling a crowd that he had dug the Grand Canyon, a small girl asked, "Where did you put all that dirt?" No answer. Legend has it that on his deathbed in 1919, Hance's last words were "I wonder where I could have put all that dirt?"

About 75 yards from the Colorado back up Red Canyon is an old camp. Hance had an asbestos mine on the north side of the river (the trailings and shaft can be seen from Hance Rapids), and the miners would spend the night in Red Canyon when packing out ore.

Tourists on horseback would take three-day trips down the Grandview Trail to camp on Horseshoe Mesa, go across to Red Can-

John Hance

David Hubbard

**The Inner Gorge**

From John W. Powell, 1895; *Canyons of the Colorado*. Reprinted by
Dover Publications, N.Y., 1961 under the title: *The Exploration of the
Colorado River and Its Canyons*.

yon via the Tonto, and then out the New Hance. Some of these early visitors carved their names below a Tapeats Sandstone ledge in Hance Canyon. Please do not deface this historic graffiti or add to it.

Hance's tourists also recorded their names and comments in his guest book at the hotel. One notable guest, William O. (Bucky) O'Neill wrote, "God made the cañon, John Hance the trails. Without the other, neither would be complete."

The red of Red Canyon is the Hakatai Shale, a Precambrian rock which is one of the layers within the Grand Canyon Supergroup (see the geology chapter). Straight across from the mouth of Red Canyon, a large basalt dike cuts across the Hakatai. Downstream the older Precambrian rocks, the Vishnu Schist and Zoroaster Granite, make their appearance as the ominous Inner Gorge. The asbestos Hance mined occurs in the Bass Limestone, another formation of the Grand Canyon Supergroup. Asbestos is an alteration product of the mineral serpentine. The serpentine is green and is seen in veins as much as a foot thick. The asbestos occurs as bands of green to yellow silky fibers up to 4 inches long within the serpentine.

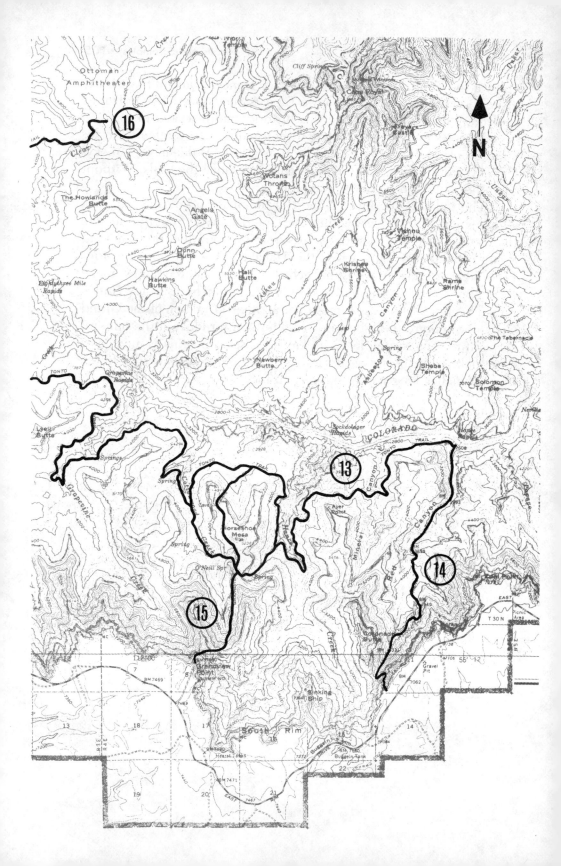

# GRAND CANYON TRAIL #15

| | |
|---|---|
| Name: | Grandview Trail |
| Trail Location: | #15 on the Index Map |
| Trailhead Elevation: | 7,400 feet |
| Total Vertical Descent: | 2,600 to top of Horseshoe Mesa |
| Length (one way): | 3 miles to Horseshoe Mesa |
| Maps: | U.S.G.S. Topos—Vishnu Temple, Grandview Point; Grand Canyon Recreational Map #4 |
| Overall Difficulty: | Moderate to Horseshoe Mesa, difficult beyond |
| Permit: | NPS |

The Grandview Trail starts down from Grandview Point. It takes about two hours to reach Horseshoe Mesa and twice that to return. There are three ways off of Horseshoe Mesa. At the southern apex of the mesa, a trail drops off the east side. It has been obscured by rockslides and is hazardous. The spring shown on the map is permanent. You will see some old mine shafts here in the Redwall. They are unsafe and contain vertical shafts . . . stay out of them. There is water in Hance Creek; hence, a good campsite.

Another way off of Horseshoe Mesa is to go out along the top of the west arm of the horseshoe. A rough trail descends a break in the Redwall.

The third trail drops off to the west into Cottonwood Canyon from the southern tip of Horseshoe Mesa. Only the spring in the west fork of the south arm of Cottonwood is dependable. O'Neill Spring and the one shown in the west arm of Cottonwood are not reliable.

A popular trip is to go down the Grandview into Cottonwood then along the Tonto Trail to the South Kaibab and out. Plan a minimum of two days. Although it does not look like it on the map, the distance from Cottonwood Creek to the Kaibab Trail is 20 miles! Do not attempt this one in hot weather.

The Hopi and possibly their ancestors, the Anasazi, used to gather blue copper ore for paint from Horseshoe Mesa in prehistoric time.

By 1892 Pete Berry along with Ralph and Niles Cameron were improving the old Indian trail so that they could mine the copper.

The ore proved to be high-grade. At the Columbian Exposition in Chicago, it was awarded a prize for being over 70% pure copper.

The "Last Chance Mine" was soon shipping out over a ton of ore per day. Several cabins and a mess hall were built on Horseshoe Mesa. The miners had many visitors so they constructed a two-story structure on the rim for tourists. The Grandview Hotel was Grand Canyon's leading tourist spot in 1895. In 1907, the bottom fell out of the copper market and the following year mining activity ceased on the mesa. Today the remains of the cookhouse and some of the cabins may be seen on the mesa. Remember that historical structures and artifacts are protected by law. Please camp at least 1/2 mile from historical sites.

After the Santa Fe Railroad constructed a spur line up to the South Rim near the Bright Angel Trail in 1901, most tourists abandoned the rough stagecoach ride to Grandview for the more easily accessible Fred Harvey accommodations.

The vegetation along this trail is typical of the South Rim routes. Back away from the rim is a well-developed ponderosa pine forest. Along the rim's edge is pinyon pine and juniper. Shrubs include scrub oak, mountain mahogany, big sagebrush, and Mormon tea. Descending off the rim, the pines give way to pale hoptree, Gambel's oak, false mock orange, single-leaf ash, Utah serviceberry, squaw bush, and fern bush. Nearing Horseshoe Mesa, the larger shrubs are replaced by blackbrush, snakeweed, four-winged saltbush, and rabbitbrush.

There are several limestone solution caves in the Redwall accessible from Horseshoe Mesa. Some of these were first explored in 1897. Flashlights and a companion are recommended. Please sign the register provided and respect the fragility of the caves. Do *not* build fires nor deface formations within the caves.

# GRAND CANYON TRAIL #16

| | |
|---|---|
| Name: | Kaibab Trail System (North, South, and Clear Creek) |
| Trail Location: | #16 on the Index Map |
| Trailhead Elevation: | North Kaibab—8,240 feet; South Kaibab—7,260 feet |
| Total Vertical Descent: | North Kaibab to Colorado River—5,760 feet<br>South Kaibab to Colorado River—4,780 feet |
| Length (one way): | North Kaibab to Colorado River—14.2 miles<br>South Kaibab to Colorado River—6.3 miles |
| Maps: | U.S.G.S. Topos—Bright Angel, Vishnu Temple; Grand Canyon Recreation Map #4 |
| Overall Difficulty | Moderate; maintained, frequently used |
| Permit: | NPS |

The Kaibab Trails along with the Bright Angel are the only regularly maintained trails within the Canyon. Hikers share these trails with mule-riders on their way to Phantom Ranch. The mules have the right-of-way and hikers are requested to stand quietly by the side of the trail and wait for instructions from the mule wrangler.

## South Kaibab Trail

The South Kaibab is often combined with the Bright Angel to provide a loop trip to Phantom Ranch and/or Bright Angel Campground at the bottom of the Grand Canyon. The Kaibab is steeper than the Bright Angel, has virtually no shade and no water, so is usually the descent route. After overnighting at the bottom, the ascent is made up the easier Bright Angel. This trip was my introduction to Canyon hiking and will probably be yours, too.

The South Kaibab begins near Yaki Point which is easily reached via paved road 4 miles east of Grand Canyon Village on the South

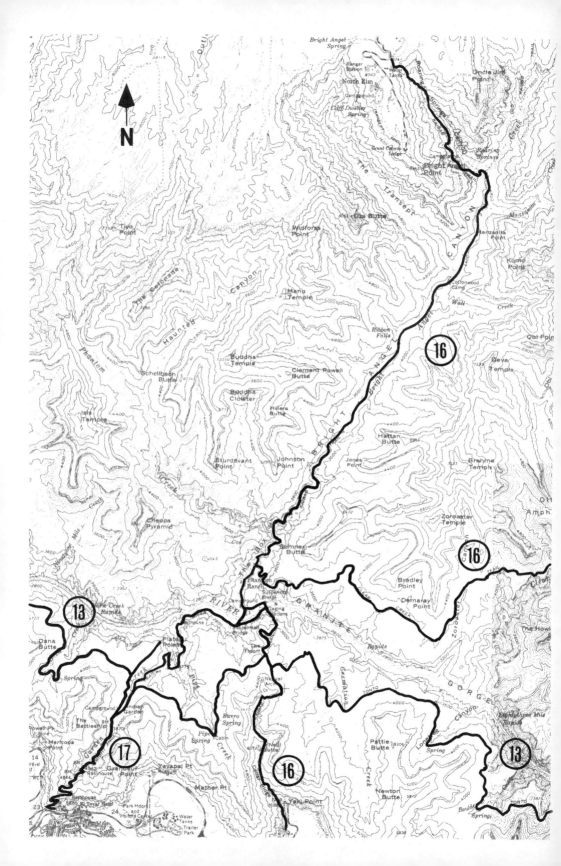

Rim. The trail quickly descends in 1.5 miles through the Kaibab, Toroweap, and Coconino Formations to Cedar Ridge. It then goes past O'Neill Butte, switchbacks down through the Supai, Redwall Limestone, and Muav to the Tonto Plateau and intersects with the Tonto Trail. The South Kaibab continues north across the Plateau to the Tipoff and then drops some 1,500 vertical feet through the Precambrian rocks. Near the Colorado River the trail is met by the River Trail (coming over from the Bright Angel). Continuing down, the trail crosses the 1928 suspension bridge to Bright Angel Campground and the tourist lodge of Phantom Ranch.

The cedars of Cedar Ridge are actually junipers, the short, shrubby trees with shredded bark and blue "berries," actually modified cones. A fossil fern exhibit is located here, as well as a toilet. Guided ranger talks to Cedar Ridge are offered during the summer.

O'Neill Butte is named after William O. (Bucky) O'Neill, onetime mayor of Prescott, Arizona, and organizer of a company of Rough Riders for duty in the Spanish-American War. He helped promote copper mining in the Grand Canyon and encouraged the building of a railroad to the South Rim.

Solution caves are passed in the Redwall limestone. And a small natural arch can be seen in the Redwall to the west from the Tonto Plateau.

An emergency phone and toilet are located near the Tipoff.

## North Kaibab Trail

The North Rim is closed due to snow usually from mid-November until mid-May. A few hardy souls have crosscountry skied or snowshoed the 45 miles from Jacob Lake to the head of the North Kaibab and then hiked across to the South Rim, another 20 miles. But most folks prefer hiking the North Kaibab during the summer and early fall.

The trailhead is located 2 miles north of the Grand Canyon Lodge on the North Entrance Road. The first 5 miles of trail quickly descend Roaring Springs Canyon to meet Bright Angel Creek. Roaring Springs, as its name suggests, can be heard long before it is seen. Water gushes out of a limestone cave and cascades down to Bright Angel Creek. Water from the springs is pumped both to the North and South Rims to serve the tourists and the Canyon residents.

The trail continues down Bright Angel Creek 2 miles to Cotton-

**Lagoon on the Kaibab**

From John W. Powell, 1895, *Canyons of the Colorado*. Reprinted by Dover Publications, N.Y., 1961 under the title: *The Exploration of the Colorado River and Its Canyons.*

wood Campground. This camping area is open during the summer only and has drinking water, restrooms, and a ranger. Fremont cottonwood trees, box elders, hornbeam, and willows line the creek banks. Also found are cattails, horsetail rush, and reeds. Look for dippers or water ouzels doing dips on rocks in the stream or "flying" underwater for insects.

Notice the vegetation away from the water. The difference is dramatic. The desert plants are widely spaced and most have leaves reduced in size and coated with wax to reduce evaporation. Common species include prickly pear and hedgehog cactus, narrow-leaf yucca, Utah agave, and mesquite.

The North Kaibab Trail continues to follow the creek and about 1.5 miles south of Cottonwood Campground passes Ribbon Falls. A bridge across Bright Angel leads to the falls. The waters of Ribbon Creek are highly mineralized with calcium carbonate derived from limestone formations above. As this mineral slowly precipitates out of solution an apron of travertine is formed behind the falls. Moss, maidenhair ferns, yellow columbines, and monkeyflower thrive in this garden spot.

Returning to the main trail, continue another 3 miles downstream to the entrance of The box. Vertical walls of black Precambrian schist rise over 1,000 feet above you. It is an awesome and gloomy place. But listen and maybe you will hear the trill of a rock wren or the descending notes and laughter of the canyon wren. On the rocks perhaps a huge chuckwalla, collared lizard, or other reptile will be sunning itself.

Another 2 miles brings you to the junction with the Clear Creek Trail. Phantom Ranch is about 1/2 mile farther, and Bright Angel Campground with drinking water, restrooms, and a ranger is just beyond the ranch.

Phantom Ranch was built in 1922 by the park service to accommodate the increasing tourist traffic to the Inner Gorge and is still the only such facility within the entire Grand Canyon. The Grand Canyon Natural History Association has a delightful booklet called *Recollections of Phantom Ranch* that delves into the fascinating history of this isolated guest ranch.

## Clear Creek Trail

The Clear Creek Trail begins about 1/2 mile north of Phantom Ranch. It climbs up out of Bright Angel Canyon and contours easterly along the Tonto Plateau 8.7 miles to Clear Creek which is perennial. There is no water between Bright Angel Creek and Clear Creek and no shade.

**Triangulation Station**

From John W. Powell, 1895; *Canyons of the Colorado*. Reprinted by Dover Publications, N.Y., 1961 under the title: *The Exploration of the Colorado River and Its Canyons.*

Back in 1903, the Kolb brothers, photographers and early residents at the South Rim, hiked over to Clear Creek to check out a prospector's story of a cliff coated with ice. They found the highest waterfall in the Grand Canyon; it falls nearly a thousand feet down the face of the Redwall Limestone and Muav Limestone and across the terraces of Bright Angel Shale. Ellsworth Kolb named the falls Cheyava, which is a Hopi word meaning intermittent.

Thirty years later, the Civilian Conservation Corps built the Clear Creek Trail. Cheyava Falls are about 4 miles upstream in the northeast arm of Clear Creek. They are most impressive in the spring when melting snows recharge the ground water.

The 3 miles down to the Colorado are also interesting. There is an 8-foot waterfall at one point, but it can be bypassed.

The entire Clear Creek area would be worthy of an extended trip to explore all of its attractions. There are a number of Indian ruins in the canyon and mescal pits where they roasted agaves. Please do not disturb these sites. The permanent water of Clear Creek attracts wildlife and it is not unusual to encounter bighorn sheep, mule deer, and a variety of smaller mammals and birds.

The trails of the Kaibab system offer an excellent introduction to Grand Canyon hiking.

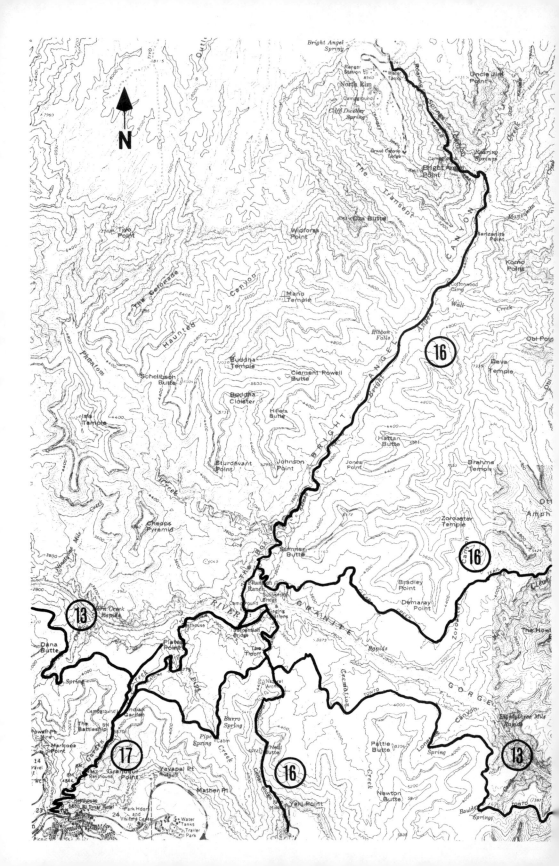

# GRAND CANYON TRAIL #17

| | |
|---|---|
| Name: | Bright Angel Trail (and River and Plateau Point Trails) |
| Trail Location: | #17 on the Index Map |
| Trailhead Elevation: | 6,860 feet |
| Total Vertical Descent: | 4,460 feet to Colorado River |
| Length (one way): | 7.5 miles to Colorado River; 9.5 miles to Phantom Ranch |
| Maps: | U.S.G.S. Topo—Bright Angel; Grand Canyon Recreational Map #4 |
| Overall Difficulty: | Moderate |
| Permit: | NPS |

The Bright Angel Trail is the best known and most used trail into the Canyon. Hikers share the path with 20 to 100 mules per day and must face urine pools and other deposits left by animals. The trail begins just west of Bright Angel Lodge in Grand Canyon Village on the South Rim. For probably a thousand years people have traveled up and down this canyon formed by the Bright Angel Fault. Along Garden Creek, prehistoric and historic Havasupai Indians raised crops of maize and beans.

Early miners soon discovered that there were more tourist dollars than gold to be found in the Canyon. So by 1903, Ralph Cameron was operating the Bright Angel as a toll trail, charging $1.00 per person. Not until 1928 did the National Park Service gain control of the trail and open it to free public access.

Up until 1930, the Bright Angel went as far as the Tonto Plateau then east along the Tonto Trail and down what is now the lower part of the South Kaibab. A primitive trail did exist directly down Garden Creek to the Colorado prior to 1930 and was used by the Kolbs and others. During the 1930's, the Civilian Conservation Corps developed the trail down Garden Creek and blasted a route along the Colorado (the River Trail) to the Kaibab Bridge.

Today, the Bright Angel Trail is more like a dirt road than a foot trail, but is still a thrill to newcomers to the Canyon. During the summer, drinking water is available 1.5 and 3 miles below the rim. At mile 4.5 is Indian Gardens Campground, which has drinking water and restrooms year-round. Plan at least four to five hours to hike from the rim to Phantom Ranch and double that time for your return.

A good day trip is to go down to Indian Gardens, out to Plateau Point (1.5 miles from Indian Gardens) and return to the rim. This is a total of 12 miles and will take all day for most hikers!

Despite all the traffic on the Bright Angel, this is still a good area for viewing bighorn sheep and mule deer. Soaring and diving along the cliff faces are violet-green swallows and the similar white-throated swifts. Ravens are usually seen riding the thermals on the lookout for scraps of food left behind by a careless hiker. Gray rock squirrels and an occasional chipmunk may also be seen begging along the trail. Please do not feed them. Artificial feeding upsets the natural behavior of these rodents.

Below Indian Gardens, Anasazi Indians farmed along Garden Creek and built granaries and dwellings in the Tapeats cliffs some 800 years ago. A little farther down the trail and the striking contact between the horizontal beds of the Tapeats Sandstone and the deformed metamorphosed Vishnu Schist is seen. This contact represents an erosional period of 300,000,000 years and is called the Great Unconformity.

The Colorado River may look inviting after a long hot, dusty trip down the trail, but beware. The river's currents are deceptive. More than one hiker has been swept away.

In 1913, former President Teddy Roosevelt descended the Bright Angel Trail on his way to the North Rim for a hunting excursion. There were still a few Havasupais living at Indian Gardens eking out an existence. Supposedly Roosevelt told these people that they had to leave the Canyon. His reasoning was that the Canyon, which he had declared a national monument in 1908, was "for the people of the nation." Apparently, he didn't feel that native Americans had any right to continue living in what was now a national playground even though they had been here for centuries.

## GRAND CANYON TRAIL #18

| | |
|---|---|
| Name: | Hermit Trail (and Waldron and Dripping Springs) |
| Trail Location: | #18 on the Index Map |
| Trailhead Elevation: | 6,700 feet |
| Total Vertical Descent: | 4,300 feet to Colorado River |
| Length (one way): | 7.7 miles rim to Hermit Creek campsite; 1.5 miles campsite to Colorado |
| Maps: | U.S.G.S. Topo—Bright Angel; Grand Canyon Recreational Map #4 |
| Overall Difficulty: | Moderate; rim to river takes 4–5 hours, return trip twice as long |
| Permit: | NPS |

The trail begins at the end of the dirt service road beyond Hermit's Rest. Hermit's Rest is at the end of the paved West Rim Drive, 8 miles west of Grand Canyon Village.

The trail quickly switchbacks through the Kaibab, Toroweap, and Coconino Formations. In the Coconino is some elaborate trail construction with slabs of sandstone layed on edge to form the base of the trail. Also on some of the sandstone slabs you will notice fossil reptile tracks. The trail enters Hermit Basin, where the first left fork, the Waldron Trail, leads back to the rim and ends at Horse Thief Tank, 2 miles distant. A nice day trip is to go down the Hermit to Hermit Basin, out the Waldron, and then cross-country back to Hermit's Rest. This loop trip is about 6 miles.

A short distance farther down Hermit Basin a second fork leads to Dripping Springs, 1.5 miles, and to the Boucher Trail. The springs flow year-round. Supposedly, Louis Boucher, the hermit, kept goldfish in a pond here. Dripping Springs makes an excellent destination for a dayhike. No camping is allowed here due to the fragility of the area.

The Hermit Trail leaves Hermit Basin and switchbacks down to Santa Maria Spring where water can be found. The wood shelter was built in 1913 when the Hermit Trail was the leading tourist trail. The trail then contours along in the Supai Formation for several miles past Fourmile Spring, which is dry, before descending through the Red-

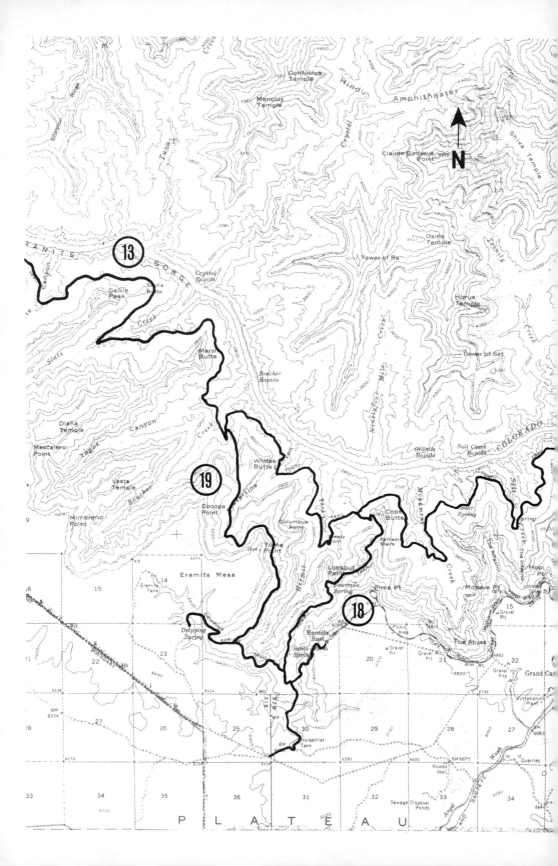

**Hermit Camp**

David Hubbard

wall at a place called the Cathedral Stairs. The trail angles down a long slope below Cope Butte and joins the Tonto Trail. Heading southwest you soon come to the site of Hermit Camp with Lookout Point forming a majestic backdrop. The Hermit Trail descends through the Tapeats Sandstone into the mica-flecked Vishnu Schist to the creek which can be followed to the Colorado. The Tonto Trail, on-the-other-hand, continues another quarter-mile along the Plateau before crossing Hermit Creek to eventually go to Boucher Canyon.

At the turn of the century, the Bright Angel Trail was privately owned. So to avoid paying toll fees, the Santa Fe Railroad decided to build their own trail into the canyon. First a road from the railroad station to Hermit's Rest had to be constructed and then a trail to the bottom of Hermit Canyon was engineered. From 1912 to 1930, the Santa Fe Railroad operated a tourist resort, Hermit Camp, on the Tonto Platform. To supply the camp a 3,000-foot cable was strung between Pima Point and Hermit Camp. A Model T Ford was lowered into the canyon but had less than a mile of road to drive on.

In 1930, the Bright Angel Trail was open to free travel and the railroad moved their tourist focus to the present village area.

The permanent water of Hermit Creek supports a lush riparian community. Coyote willow, desert broom, arroweed, and salt cedar are the common shrubs. Mesquite, catclaw, and prickly pear cactus are also common. Red-spotted toads and canyon treefrogs are frequently seen in quiet pools. Yellow monkeyflowers appear in the spring.

The park service has designated camping sites for you to use. This is to help preserve the delicate streamside ecology.

A nice weekend trip is to go down the Hermit, across the Tonto to Indian Gardens, and out the Bright Angel. Bighorn sheep are often encountered, sometimes remarkably close, along this stretch of the Tonto.

# GRAND CANYON TRAIL #19

| | |
|---|---|
| Name: | Boucher Trail |
| Trail Location: | #19 on the Index Map |
| Trailhead Elevation: | 6,640 feet |
| Total Vertical Descent: | 3,840 feet to Boucher Creek |
| Length (one way): | About 9 miles from Hermit's Rest to Boucher Creek |
| Maps: | U.S.G.S. Topo—Bright Angel; Grand Canyon Recreational Map #4 |
| Overall Difficulty: | Difficult |
| Permit: | NPS |

The original trailhead can be reached via a poor dirt road south of Eremita Mesa. However it is much easier just to go down the Hermit Trail and then cross over to the Boucher via the Dripping Springs Trail (see Grand Canyon Trail #18). A sign marks the junction of the Boucher with Dripping Springs. The Boucher contours along the base of the Hermit Shale and the top of the Supai on the west side of Hermit Canyon. Keep a sharp eye open for beautiful fern fossils in the red shale.

About 1 mile beyond Columbus Point, the trail begins to descend through the Supai and goes southwest toward the head of Travertine Canyon. Near the head of Travertine, the trail descends steeply to the top of the Redwall. You may not follow an actual trail here but rather a talus slope. No matter. Once on the Redwall Limestone, traverse along the west side of Travertine Canyon to the saddle south of White's Butte. The trail off the west side of this saddle is very steep and covered with loose rocks. Watch your step.

The Tonto Trail is encountered just before reaching Boucher Creek, which flows year-round. It is possible to walk down the creek 2 miles to the Colorado River. Plan five to six hours of waterless hiking from Hermit's Rest to Boucher Creek; double that time for the trip out.

The low rock-walled ruin near the junction of the trail with the creek is all that remains of Louis D. Boucher's "The Hermit" cabin.

Boucher came to the Grand Canyon about 1891 to seek his fortune. He had one camp at Dripping Springs where he kept, besides his horses and mules, goldfish in a trough. He called the trail

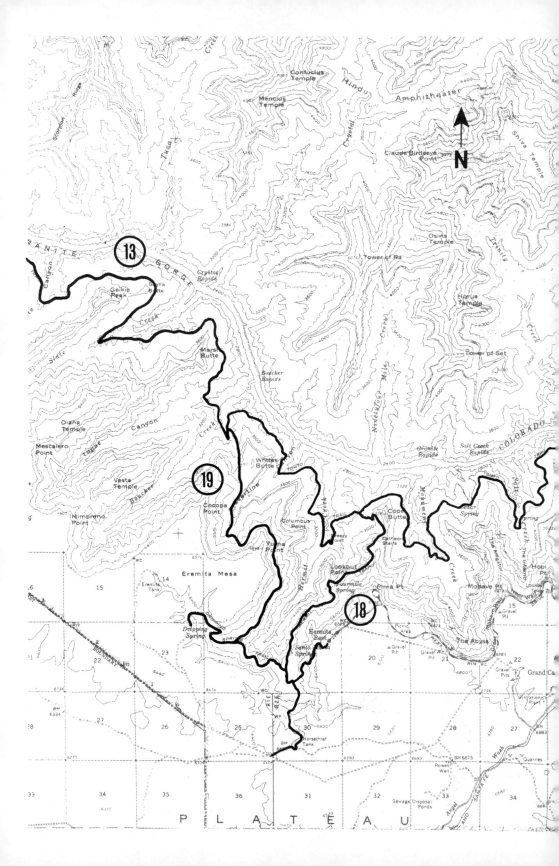

**Louis Boucher**

David Hubbard

that he built from here to Long (Boucher) Canyon the Silver Bell, perhaps after the bell that hung from his white mule's neck. Along Boucher Creek, he planted 75 trees, including orange, fig, peach, pear, apricot, apple, nectarine, and pomegranate. He also raised tomatoes, chili, cucumbers, melons, and grapes. Nearby was his copper mine—but he never struck it rich—so in 1912, he moved to Utah.

A delightful three-day or longer hike is to go down the Boucher, then exit along the Tonto, and out the Hermit.

Feral burros, descendants of animals released by prospectors, used to be quite common in this area. Their numerous trails and overgrazing have scarred much of the Tonto Platform. At this time, the park service has apparently been successful at removing these exotic animals from the Canyon.

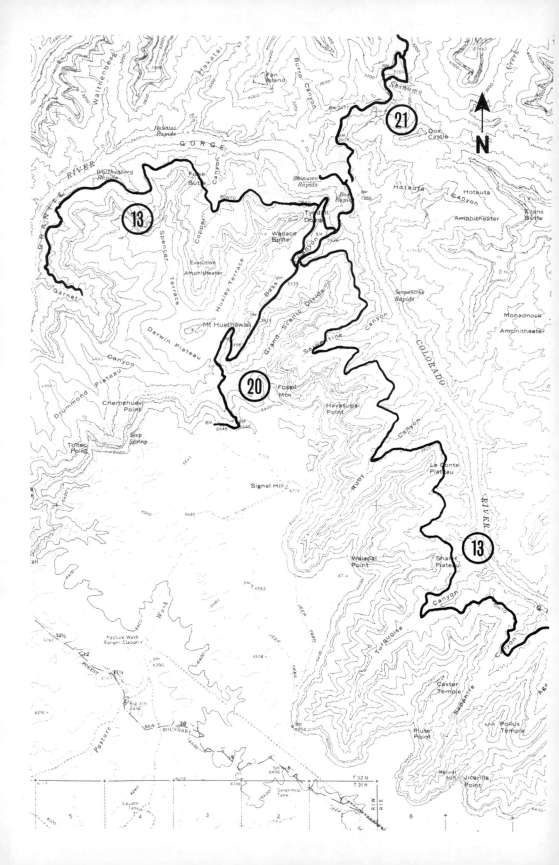

# GRAND CANYON TRAIL #20

| | |
|---|---|
| Name: | South Bass Trail |
| Trail Location: | #20 on the Index Map |
| Trailhead Elevation: | 6,650 feet |
| Total Vertical Descent: | 4,400 feet |
| Length (one way): | About 7 miles rim to river |
| Maps: | U.S.G.S. Topo—Havasupai Point; |
| | Grand Canyon Recreational Map #5 |
| Overall Difficulty: | Difficult |
| Permit: | NPS |

This trailhead is located about 4 miles north of the Pasture Wash Ranger Station. There are a couple of routes to the ranger station. It is best to check with the park service backcountry office about the condition of the approach roads. Sometimes a four-wheel drive vehicle is necessary.

The Bass Trail used to be confused by game and feral burro trails but it has become quite distinct in recent years through more use by hikers. The trail begins by angling eastward down through the Kaibab and Toroweap Formations and then switchbacking through the Coconino Sandstone. The trail then heads toward Mt. Huethawali across the Esplanade, a relatively broad platform or bench formed by the Esplanade Sandstone, the upper formation of the Supai Group.

Mystic Springs shown on older maps on the northwest side of Mt. Huethawali (and deleted on newer revisions because the cartographer thought the spring had dried up) is actually farther from the butte on the narrowest part of the neck leading to Spencer Terrace. It would mean a 2-mile or so round trip detour to visit this spring. The only water *on* the Bass Trail is at the Colorado River!

Cairns mark the descent off the Esplanade. The trail has been washed out in places but the route is still obvious. The trail leads south to the head of Bass Canyon and eventually turns to the northeast and contours along the east side of the canyon.

If you want to take the Tonto Trail over to Garnet Canyon (see Grand Canyon Trail #13), head northwest when you are southeast of Wallace Butte. You will soon cross the Tonto or a path leading to it. It is a long, hot walk to Garnet; plan at least five hours. There is water in Garnet, but it is saline. You will have to make your way down the canyon to the river for a cool drink.

The Tonto Trail to Boucher also takes off southeast of Wallace Butte. It is 22 mostly dry miles to Boucher. The Tonto is indistinct in places and seems to be endless as it contours in and out of each little wash and drainage.

The Bass Trail continues down the streambed until almost reaching the river. If you continue all the way to the river, you are cliffed-out. So stay alert and you will notice the trail climbing out of the streambed and heading west. In about a third of a mile, a rock cairn marks a short but steep break in the cliffs to the river at Bass Rapids. Or you may continue another third of a mile west and get down to the river at Shinumo Rapids. Plan about five hours to descend the Bass Trail and almost double that to go out.

William Bass learned from the Havasupai Indians about Trail Canyon, now called Bass, and its route from the rim to the river. Bass had come west in 1883 for his health at the age of 34. Doctors were sure he didn't have long to live. He was so taken with the splendor of the Grand Canyon that he started a tourist business on the rim. He would take visitors down to the river and cross the Colorado in a small boat (later he installed a cable with a cage big enough to hold a burro) to a camp and garden on the bank of Shinumo Creek.

He improved a trail that a prospector named White had built coming down from the North Rim and took hunting parties up on the Kaibab Plateau.

In 1894, Bass married one of the tourists, a music teacher from New York, Ada Diefendorf. Life at Bass Camp at the head of the trail lacked most luxuries including running water. To do laundry, Ada would sometimes carry the dirty clothes down to Shinumo Creek, a three-day round trip. But the hard life must have agreed with William for he lived to be 84 years old.

Near where Bass used to cross the river lies a metal boat. One story says that Bert Loper, the grand old man of the river, built it in 1914 at Green River, Utah. A river party abandoned it in 1915.

You probably noticed on the topo map a trail leading west off of the Bass on the Esplanade. Apparently, this was a trail being built by a Havasupai to connect his home in Supai with the Bass Trail. He only got as far as Forester Canyon. It is interesting to explore the Esplanade, but the Havasupai have closed the rim area to non-Indians so you cannot exit at Apache Point as shown on the topo map without their consent.

### The Colorado River

From John W. Powell, 1895; *Canyons of the Colorado*. Reprinted by Dover Publications, N.Y., 1961 under the title: *The Exploration of the Colorado River and Its Canyons*.

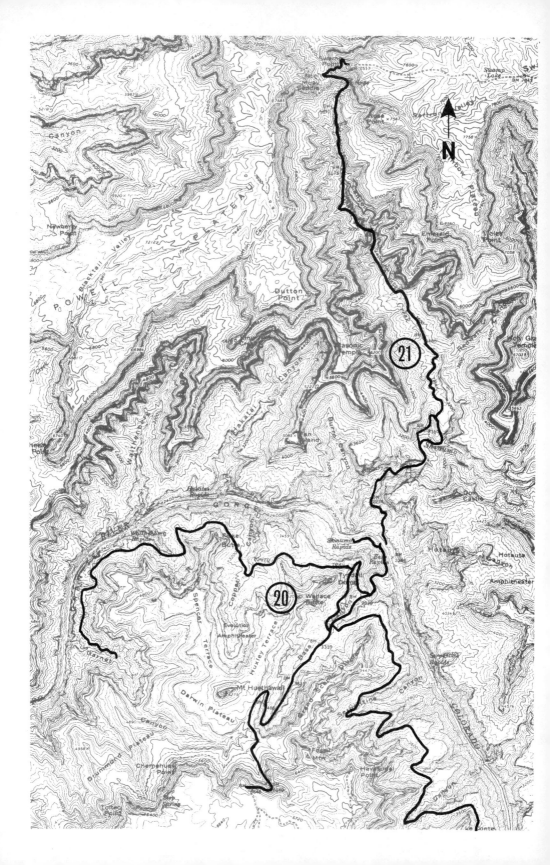

# GRAND CANYON TRAIL #21

| | |
|---|---|
| Name: | North Bass (Shinumo Creek) Trail |
| Trail Location: | #21 on the Index Map |
| Trailhead Elevation: | 7,500 feet |
| Total Vertical Descent: | 5,300 feet |
| Length (one way): | About 14 miles rim to river |
| Maps: | U.S.G.S. Topos—Powell Plateau, Havasupai Point; Grand Canyon Recreational Map #5 |
| Overall Difficulty: | Very rugged; consider 3 to 4 days for round trip |
| Permit: | NPS |

About 1 mile south of the Kaibab Lodge turn west off Highway 67 onto Forest Service Road #422. Turn left onto Forest Service Road #270. Drive about 2 miles and take the second major right at Forest Service Road #233. Go left onto Forest Service Road #233A; go past Tipover Spring to Swamp Ridge Road. Continue out to Swamp Point and the trailhead.

The trail drops down into Muav Saddle then turns eastward to a spring at the base of the Coconino Sandstone. The route goes down a steep talus slope to the bottom of Muav Canyon. As you approach the Redwall Limestone, the trail veers to the west side of the canyon. Once out of the streambed, the trail crosses three small saddles before reaching the top of the Redwall. A large crain marks the route down through the Redwall but be sure to study the map closely. At the base of the Redwall there is usually water in White Creek. Follow the creek until you are near the Tapeats Sandstone. Here the trail begins to climb up the west slope. As the trail begins to go back down through the Tapeats at a point overlooking Shinumo Creek, you may want to detour off the trail as shown on the topo and take a more direct and easier burro trail east of the benchmark with the elevation 3,150. Consult your map.

Shinumo Creek is a permanent stream and is home to some trout and water ouzels or dippers. Continue down the creek. About a mile before coming to the Colorado, the trail turns south up and over a ridge to a fairly open terrace. It was here that engineer Robert Stanton thought a switchyard for his railroad through the Grand Canyon could be built. (See Grand Canyon Trail #7.)

Towering above Shinumo Creek is the immense Powell Plateau. In 1907, a struggling author by the name of Zane Grey came out West to experience firsthand the adventure of the frontier. Grey, C.J. "Buffalo" Jones, and James Emett, a ferryman from Lee's Ferry, made a trip to the remote Powell Plateau to lasso lions alive for zoos in the East. They succeeded in roping and transporting on horseback several very angry mountain lions.

# GRAND CANYON TRAIL #22

Name:                          Thunder River (Bill Hall and Deer
                               Creek Trails)
Trail Location:                #22 on the Index Map
Trailhead Elevation:           7,200 feet at Monument Point
Total Vertical Descent:        5,250 feet to Colorado River at
                               Tapeats Rapid
Length (one way):              About 12 miles from Monument Point
                               to Tapeats Rapid
Maps:                          U.S.G.S. Topos—Kanab Point,
                               Powell Plateau
Overall Difficulty:            Moderate but long; no water until
                               Thunder River
Permit:                        NPS

About 1 mile south of the Kaibab Lodge in Demotte Park turn west off of Highway 67 onto Forest Service Road #422. Drive 20 miles and then turn left on the Indian Hollow Road, Forest Service Road #425. At Big Saddle Camp turn left (south) on Forest Service Road #292A and follow the signs to Monument Point. Total driving distance from lodge to rim is about 36 miles.

If you had gone right at Big Saddle Camp, you would have ended up at Indian Hollow Campground and the head of the Thunder River Trail. However, by starting at Monument Point, you will save yourself about 5 miles of walking. This shortcut is called the Bill Hall Trail.

The Bill Hall Trail drops off the eastern tip of Monument Point then swings around to the west and drops steeply down to the Esplanade where it intersects the Thunder River Trail coming from Indian Hollow Campground. This is a good spot to cache water for the return trip.

The trail is faint in places but well-marked by rock cairns. The trail switchbacks down into Surprise Valley. Although you have just hiked down through the Supai and Redwall Formations, the bottom of the "Valley" is once again Supai. Over a cubic mile of rock has slid or slumped downward.

A large cairn marks the turnoff to Deer Creek; more about this

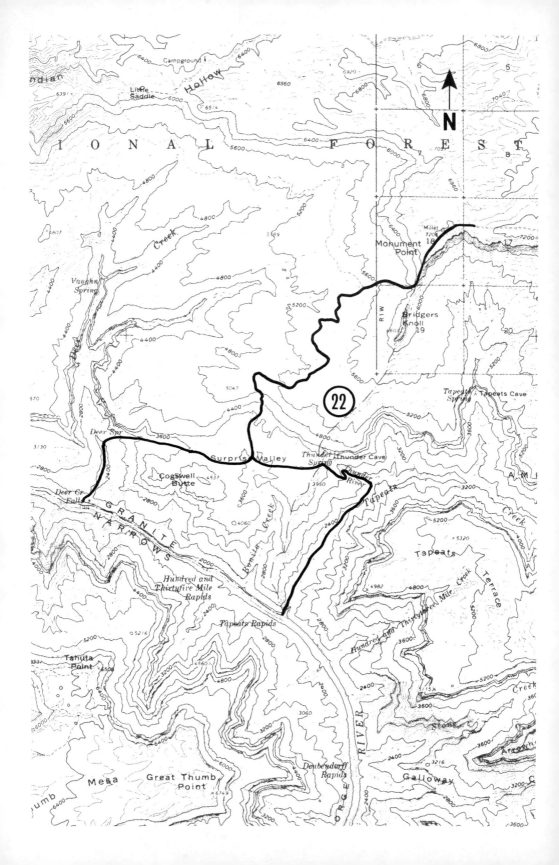

later. The Thunder River Trail turns east, crosses the "Valley," and you get your first glimpse of Thunder River gushing out of a Muav Limestone cave. By this time you are no doubt hot and thirsty and the shade of the cottonwoods and willows is very inviting. Remember, though, that there is no camping allowed along Thunder River due to the sensitivity of the riparian habitat.

Experienced cavers have entered the cave and explored underground channels and cascades. It is a dangerously slippery climb to the cave's mouth and I do not recommend attempting it.

Thunder River may be the world's shortest river in that it cascades only about a half-mile before emptying into Tapeats Creek. A designated campsite is found on the east side of Tapeats. The hike from Monument Point to this camp takes about seven hours. To reach the Colorado some 2 miles away, continue down the east side of the creek staying low near creek level. Cross the creek to the west side before it plunges into a narrow granite gorge; this point is marked with rock cairns on both sides of the creek. The trail follows along the gorge until it overlooks the river confluence. Here it descends steeply. Count on over an hour from the camp to the river because of the route's difficulty and creek crossings. Remember, too, that at times, especially during the spring run-off, Tapeats Creek may be *impossible* to cross. Another designated campsite exists near the confluence.

Scattered along Tapeats Creek are prehistoric Indian ruins of Cohonina origin. That makes them about a thousand years old. Please do not disturb them. You will also notice uprooted old cottonwood trees, the aftermath of recent flash flooding.

Instead of going down to the Colorado, you can go up Tapeats Creek. This is only feasible when the creek is low because much of your time is spent wading in the water. Like Thunder River, Tapeats also issues forth from a cave. The Tapeats cave is filled with ice-cold water and should not be entered.

Let's return to Surprise Valley and the turn-off to Deer Creek. It is about 3.5 miles or two hours to Deer Creek from Surprise Valley. The trail skirts to the north above Deer Spring before reaching the creek. Deer Creek is a wonderful Eden of cottonwoods and willows. Unfortunately careless people have started several wild fires in the area in the past few years.

A short walk down Deer Creek brings you to some spectacular narrows in the Tapeats Sandstone and a 100-foot-plus waterfall plunging practically into the Colorado River. A trail descends to the river

**Deer Creek Falls**

David Hubbard

just west of the falls. No camping is allowed at the base of the falls and designated sites exist in upper Deer Creek.

Remember that these riparian areas are particularly fragile. Stay on established trails, camp where the park service suggests, do not bathe or wash dishes in the streams, and be careful with fire.

This trail system was originally discovered by the prehistoric Cohonina and later used by Paiutes, including a fellow named Ta Pits. In 1876, prospectors came looking for gold and improved the trails for stock over the next decade. The U.S. Forest Service improved the Thunder River Trail in 1926.

# GRAND CANYON TRAIL #23

| | |
|---|---|
| Name: | Kanab Canyon |
| Trail Location: | #23 on the Index Map |
| Trailhead Elevation: | 5,300 feet at Hack's Canyon |
| Total Vertical Descent: | 3,380 feet to Colorado River |
| Length (one way): | About 21 miles from Hack's Canyon to Colorado River; plan at least 3 days one way |
| Maps: | U.S.G.S. Topos—Jumpup Canyon, Kanab Point, Heaton Knolls |
| Overall Difficulty: | Moderate to difficult |
| Permit: | NPS south of Jumpup Canyon; no permit required north |

Kanab Canyon is one of the largest side canyons to the Grand. Its headwaters are on the Paunsaugunt Plateau in Utah, some 100 miles north. There are a number of trails that lead into Kanab Canyon. Most of them date back to the late 1800's and early 1900's when cowboys began to graze their cows in the Canyon.

John Wesley Powell, the first scientific explorer of the Colorado River, ended his 1872 river expedition at Kanab Canyon. And now, a hundred years later, uranium prospectors are searching for the radioactive ore (north of the park boundary).

Hack's Canyon is one popular way into Kanab. Take Highway 389 8 miles west of Fredonia. Turn south onto B.L.M. Road #59, the road to Toroweap. Follow this dirt road approximately 17 miles and turn left (southeast) by an old corral. Head in the general direction between Hack's and Grama Canyons. You should pass an abandoned ranch, go through three gates, and you should hit the north rim of Hack's above Black Willow Spring. Here a trail descends into the canyon.

Kanab Canyon and its many side canyons are fascinating to explore. The higher elevations support pinyon pine and juniper, Gambel's oak, boxelder, big-tooth maple, New Mexico locust, and purple asters. As you descend, these plants give way to Fremont cottonwood, desert willow, Apache plume, pricklypear, catclaw, shrub live oak, Mormon tea, yucca, and agave.

The riparian or streamside vegetation has suffered in the upper

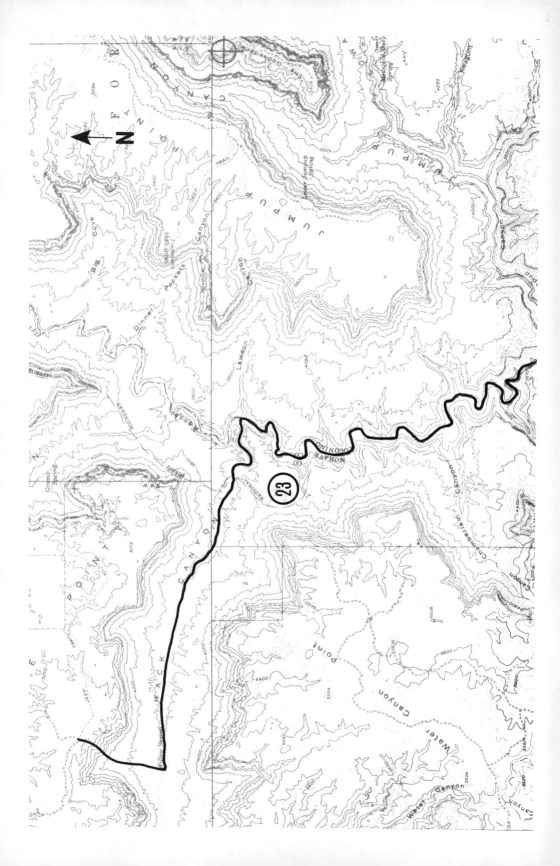

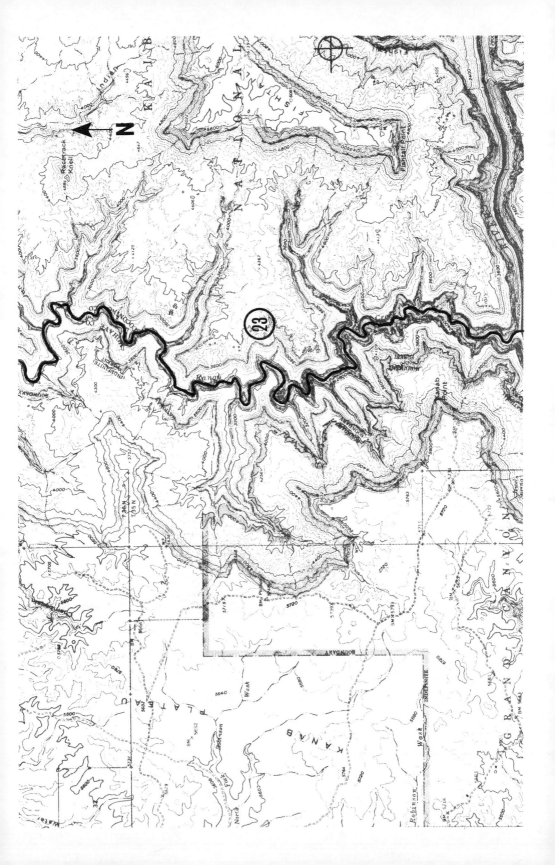

**Kanab Canyon, in the Redwall Limestone**

From John W. Powell, 1895; *Canyons of the Colorado*. Reprinted by
Dover Publications, N.Y., 1961 under the title: *The Exploration of the
Colorado River and Its Canyons*.

reaches of Kanab due to diversion of Kanab Creek by farmers in Fredonia and overgrazing. Today uranium mining threatens the upper drainages.

Below Kanab Canyon's junction with Jumpup Canyon the stream has cut a narrow gorge in the Redwall Limestone. Here redbud makes its appearance. Clinging here and there on the canyon walls are ancient floodplains supporting catclaw, pricklypear, Russian thistle (also known as tumbleweed, an exotic plant accidentally introduced in the late 1800's throughout the West), and grasses.

About 2 miles south of the Jumpup and Kanab junction, springs issue from the steambed and left bank and mark the beginning of the permanent portion of Kanab Creek. Another mile and a half and Hanging Gardens is reached. John Wesley Powell named this Shower-Bath Spring in 1872. The permanent flow supports desert willow, salt cedar or tamarisk, blanketflower, asters, monkeyflowers, maidenhair ferns, common reed, satintail, datura, and grasses. Farther downstream are found Virginia creeper, more redbud trees, the exotic Russian olive tree, catclaw, wire lettuce, evening primrose, lobeleaf groundsel, cane bluestem, netleaf hackberry, rocknettle, and wolfberry. On the ledges and talus slopes grow hedgehog cactus and barrel cactus up to 4 feet tall.

Sometimes in the leaf litter along the stream are found the land snail *Oreohelix yavapai*. Canyon treefrogs frequent the secluded pools and an occasional Great Basin rattlesnake may be encountered. This rattlesnake is not as common as the pink Grand Canyon rattlesnake.

Kanab Canyon is home for many birds. Some to look for include blue-winged teal, pintail, turkey vulture, white-throated swift, belted kingfisher, red-shafted flicker, yellow-bellied sapsucker, Steller's jay, scrub jay, common raven, mountain chickadee, dipper, house wren, canyon wren, yellowthroat, Wilson's warbler, Scott's oriole, lesser goldfinch, green-tailed towhee, white-crowned sparrow, and loggerhead shrike.

Bighorn sheep, mountain lion, muledeer, coyote, bats, and canyon mice haunt this area.

Kanab Canyon and its tributaries offer many days of pleasant exploration.

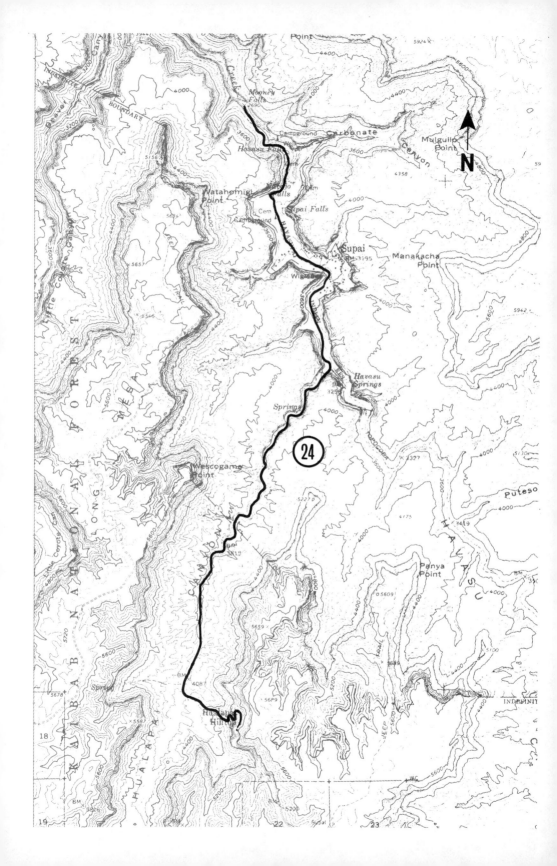

# GRAND CANYON TRAIL #24

| | |
|---|---|
| Name: | Hualapai Hilltop Trail (Supai Trail) |
| Trail Location: | #24 on the Index Map |
| Trailhead Elevation: | 5,200 feet |
| Total Vertical Descent: | 2,000 feet to Supai Village |
| Length (one way): | About 8 miles to Supai Village |
| Maps: | U.S.G.S. Topos—Supai, Kanab Point, Tuckup Canyon |
| Overall Difficulty: | Easy to moderate, maintained trail |
| Permit: | Havasupai Tourist Enterprise |

This popular trail is reached by taking a road about 7 miles east of Peach Springs. It is a little over 60 miles to the trailhead and most of the road is now paved. The trail is easy to follow. Hordes of tourists make the trip annually. Still, Havasu Canyon is one of the most beautiful places within the Grand Canyon. Reservations are necessary for the campground. There is a modest fee for entering the reservation and a charge for camping. For the latest information write the Havasupai Tourist Enterprise, Supai, Arizona 86435 or call (602) 448-2121.

The Havasupai people have lived in the Grand Canyon for centuries. Traditionally, they would spend the summers along Havasu Creek and other permanent streams growing maize, beans, and squash. Agaves, also called mescal or century plants, would be dug up and roasted. During the winter, they lived on the rim and hunted mule deer and rabbits. Pinyon nuts and other wild foods would be gathered.

This annual migration was stopped in the summer of 1880 when the Federal government established a reservation for the Havasupai in the bottom of Havasu Canyon. The original reservation was a tract of land about 5 miles wide and 12 long where about 200 people were living. The government did not make any provisions for the annual migration to the rim country. Nor did the Havasupais immediately comprehend the idea of a reservation. For nearly a century, the Havasupai battled in the courts to regain some of their traditional land. Finally, in 1975, the reservation was enlarged to include some of the highlands. The poigant story of this struggle is told in Stephen Hirst's *Life in a Narrow Place*. This book will give you some insight

143

into the problems of the reservation system and an intimate look at the past and present lifestyle of these interesting canyon people.

On some older maps and in other guidebooks, other trails into Havasupai may be mentioned. At this time, these other trails are closed to non-Indian use. Only the Hualapai Hilltop Trail is open to tourists.

# GRAND CANYON TRAIL #25

| | |
|---|---|
| Name: | Tuckup Trail (Tuweep Trail)  ✓ |
| Trail Location: | #25 on the Index Map |
| Trailhead Elevation: | 4,500 feet |
| Length (one way): | 64 miles to Boysag Point |
| Maps: | U.S.G.S. Topos—Tuckup Canyon, Kanab Canyon, Mt. Trumbell SE, Vulcan's Throne |
| Overall Difficulty: | Difficult; previous canyon experience necessary |
| Permit: | NPS |

The trail begins near the Toroweap Ranger Station (see Trail #26 for driving directions). From the ranger station drive south toward the Toroweap Overlook. There is a turnoff to the left (east) in about 5 miles. Follow this road to its end and you will be on the Tuckup Trail. Check with the ranger as to the best place to leave your vehicle.

The Tuckup Trail is indistinct and meanders across the Esplanade some 64 miles to Boysag Point. It exits the Canyon at the head of Hundred and Fifty Mile Canyon. One can continue hiking cross-country on the Esplanade all the way to Hack's Canyon another 50 miles or so.

A trail comes down from the rim southwest of Schmutz Spring in upper Tuckup Canyon and breaks the Tuckup Trail into two roughly equal segments. Driving to the head of this side trail or to the head of Hundred and Fifty Mile Canyon can be quite an adventure in route finding. If you can't use a topo map and if you haven't developed that sixth sense one needs to drive the backroads of the Arizona Strip country, then you shouldn't be out there. Hike the Bright Angel instead.

But for experienced canyon hikers, the solitude and immensity of space that this trail offers makes the route-finding effort worth it. Don't be surprised if you encounter a few cows or even a couple of cowboys. There are several life tenure grazing permits for this area which were granted when this land was designated a national monument in 1932 (it was incorporated into the national park in 1975).

Park Service literature claims that Schmutz, June, and Cotton-

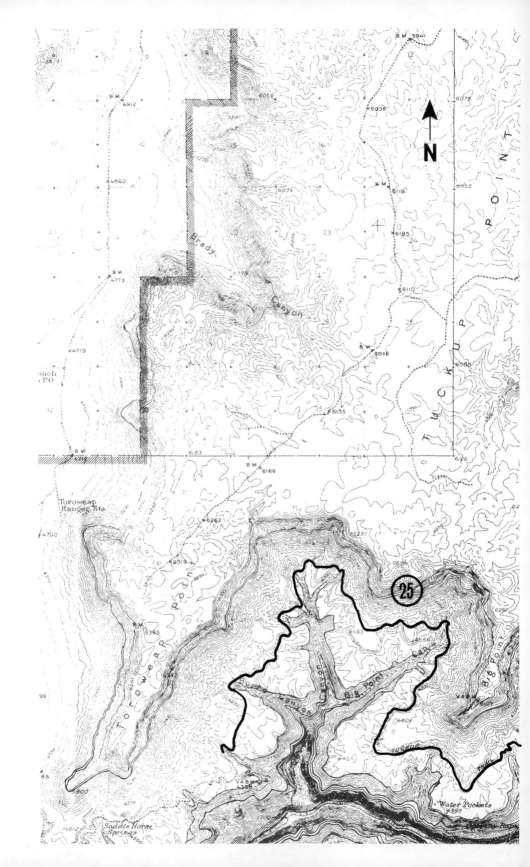

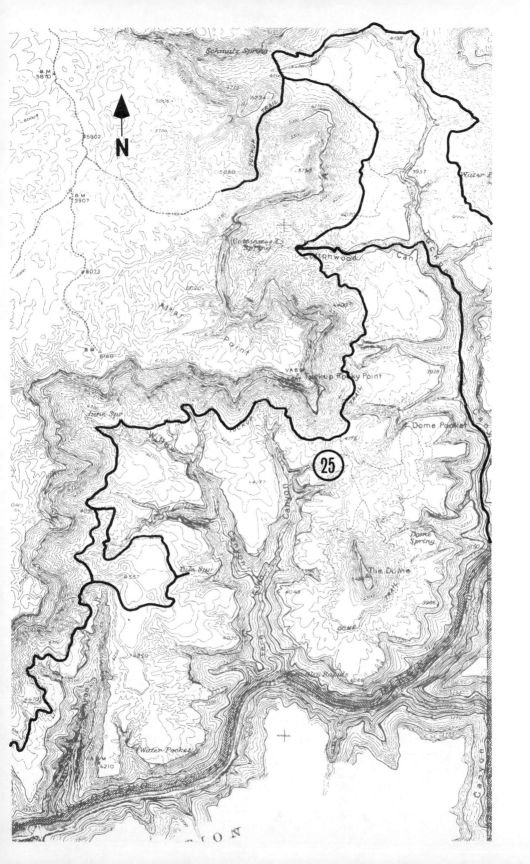

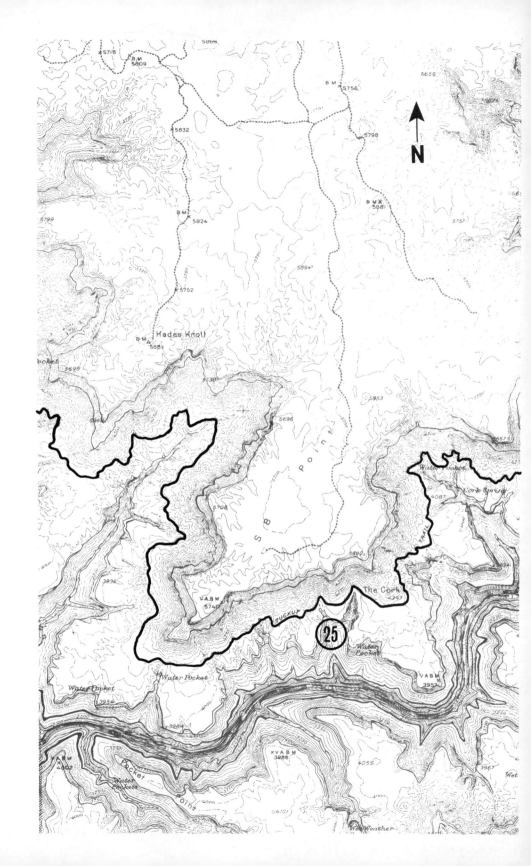

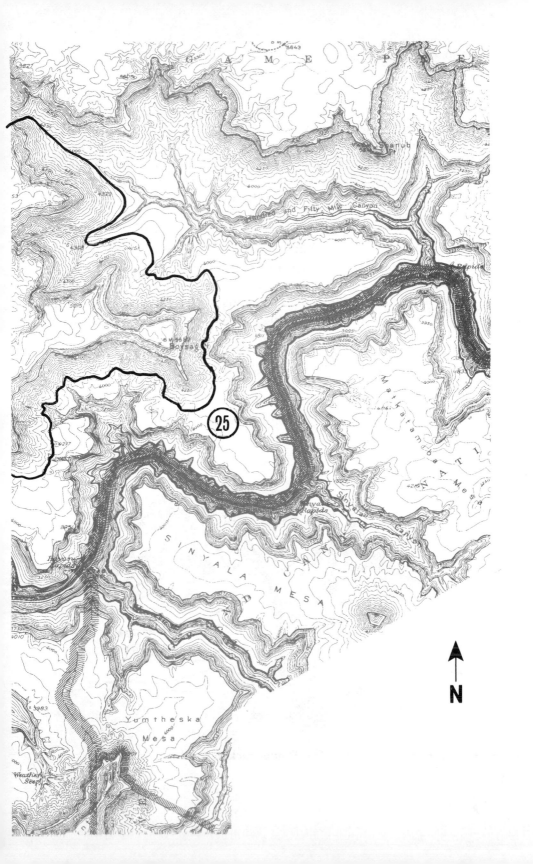

wood Springs are dependable. The latter two *may* be; however, Schmutz was dry in the spring of 1977. Tule, Cork, and Dome may contain water after a heavy winter. And after a heavy rain, potholes in the Supai Formation will hold water for a few days.

A loop trip is possible by descending Cottonwood Canyon into Tuckup Canyon. Then go down Tuckup to the Colorado, hiking along the bank to the Lava Falls Trail (Grand Canyon Trail #26) and out. Plan at least a week for this rugged hike. There are two places (one in Cottonwood and one in Tuckup) where the security of a rope belay may be welcomed. The huge chockstone near the mouth of Tuckup may seem impossible except to those willing to rappel 50 feet. But rappelling is not necessary. Instead go west, up and out of the canyon floor, and follow a dim trail. This leads to a steep but easily climbed cliff which takes you down to the canyon floor below the chockstone. A 40-foot rope to use as a handline is helpful.

Tuckup Canyon is full of surprises, including narrow side canyons and a natural bridge composed of a conglomerate spanning the canyon.

**The Dome-Tuckup Trail**

David Hubbard

# GRAND CANYON TRAIL #26

| | |
|---|---|
| Name: | Lava Falls Trail |
| Trail Location: | #26 on the Index Map |
| Trailhead Elevation: | 4,000 feet |
| Total Vertical Descent: | 2,325 feet |
| Length (one way): | 1.5 miles |
| Maps: | U.S.G.S. Topo—Vulcan's Throne |
| Overall Difficulty: | Steep, hazardous |
| Permit: | NPS |

This trailhead is located in the remote Torowcap Valley in the Arizona Strip country. To reach this spot drive west of Fredonia on Highway 389 toward Pipe Springs National Monument, an old Mormon fort. About 8 miles out of town turn south onto B.L.M. Road #59. Follow this dirt road to the Toroweap Ranger Station, approximately 55 miles. Continue south another 3.5 miles and the road forks. The left fork leads another 2.5 miles to the Toroweap Overlook, a spectacular view of the Colorado River 3,000 feet below. The right fork takes you along the west side of Vulcan's Throne, the large extinct volcanic cone directly ahead. The road goes *through* Toroweap Lake which is usually dry. If not dry, do not attempt to drive across. Instead walk around the lake or sometimes it is possible to drive around the north side of the water. The road ends on the southwest side of Vulcan's Throne and the Lava Trail begins.

Don't let the shortness of this trail deceive you. The term trail is used loosely. To follow the route you must go from cairn to cairn. To confuse matters lost hikers have built additional cairns which may lead you astray. Just remember that although the trail is steep and rocky there is no need for rappelling or actual rock climbing (a distinct possibility on some of the incorrectly marked routes). Figure at least two hours to descend and four hours for the return trip.

The main attraction of this trail other than the view is Lava Falls Rapid. On a scale of 1 to 10, with 10 being the most difficult, Lava Falls is rated by many boatmen as 10+. The river drops over 30 feet in a fury of whitewater. Quite a few river runners flip boats here.

Beginning about 1 million years ago, a series of basaltic lava flows filled Toroweap Valley and spilled into the Grand Canyon damming the Colorado River. Powell said of this event, "What a

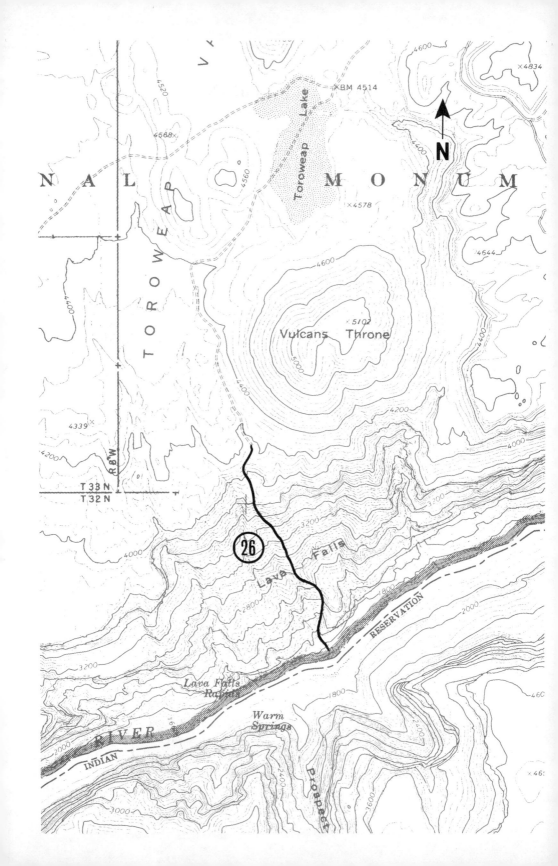

conflict of water and fire there must have been here! Just imagine a river of molten rock running down into a river of melted snow. What a seething and boiling of the waters; what clouds of steam rolled into the heavens!"

The impounded waters eventually spilled over the lava dam and slowly eroded it away. The dam's remnants and boulders washed in from Prospect Canyon have created this rapid.

This route was known to the prehistoric Indians and a number of ancient ceramic pots have been discovered in caves nearby. Perhaps these people swam across the quiet stretch of river above the rapid and then hiked out Prospect Canyon. It is known that Paiutes traveled back and forth across the Colorado and this would have been a good route.

**Raft in Lava Falls**

David Hubbard

**Grand Canyon at the Foot of the Toroweap, Looking East**

From John W. Powell, 1895; *Canyons of the Colorado*. Reprinted by
Dover Publications, N.Y., 1961 under the title: *The Exploration of the
Colorado River and Its Canyons*.

**Recent Lava Flow on the Uinkaret**

From John W. Powell, 1895; *Canyons of the Colorado*. Reprinted by Dover Publications, N.Y., 1961 under the title: *The Exploration of the Colorado River and Its Canyons.*

# GRAND CANYON TRAIL #27

| | |
|---|---|
| Name: | Whitmore Wash Trail |
| Trail Location: | #27 on the Index Map |
| Trailhead Elevation: | 2,500 feet |
| Total Vertical Descent: | 920 feet |
| Length (one way): | .75 mile |
| Maps: | U.S.G.S. Topo—Whitmore Rapids |
| Overall Difficulty: | Easy |
| Permit: | NPS |

The easiest way to reach this trail (if there is an easy way) is to take B.L.M. Road 59 from St. George, Utah to the ghost town of Mt. Trumbull (see driving directions for Grand Canyon Trail #28), and

**Whitmore Wash Trail**

David Hubbard

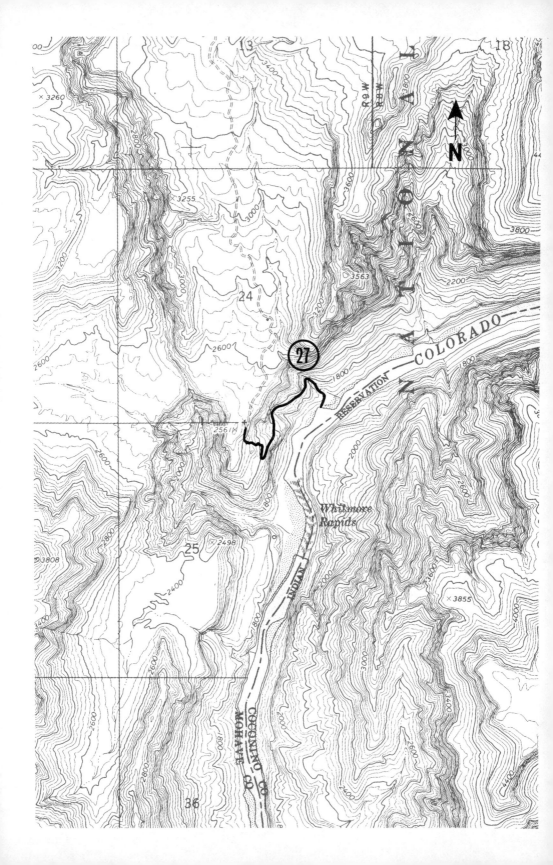

from there southward through Whitmore Canyon. At the road's end a good trail descends to the Colorado River.

Whitmore was named for a St. George, Utah man who had a ranch near Mt. Trumbull on the Uinkaret Plateau, and who was visited by Frederick Dellenbaugh, a member of the second Powell Expedition in 1872.

Here the Redwall Limestone and Muav Limestone are separated by over 300 feet of Temple Butte limestones and dolomites. Basaltic lava flows have filled Whitmore Wash to the level of the Esplanade. In many places the basalt fractured into patterns called columnar jointing as it cooled.

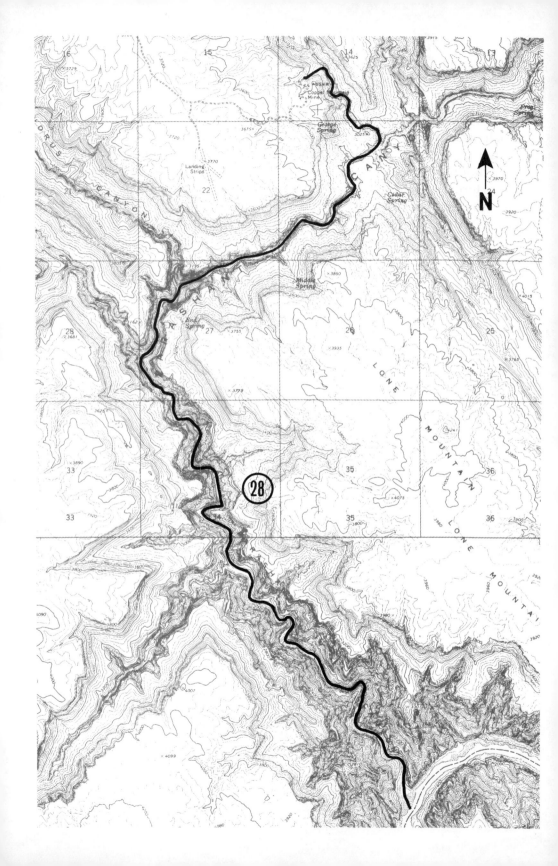

# GRAND CANYON TRAIL #28

| | |
|---|---|
| Name: | Parashant Canyon |
| Trail Location: | #28 on the Index Map |
| Trailhead Elevation: | 3,320 feet |
| Total Vertical Descent: | 1,800 feet |
| Length (one way): | About 10 miles |
| Maps: | U.S.G.S. Topos—Whitmore Point, Whitmore Point SE |
| Overall Difficulty: | Moderate |
| Permit: | NPS |

From the Main Street in St. George, Utah, go south on street 700 East. Go past Dixie College and turn left on 400 East. Pass under Interstate 15 and in another half-mile the road takes a sharp bend to the right. After another half mile you will cross the Virgin River. Stay right on the paved road. The asphalt ends at the Utah/Arizona state line. Twenty-one miles from the state line you will come to a major intersection. The right fork goes west into the Blackrock Mountain area. Take the left fork to Mt. Trumbull. Another 19 miles and another major road fork is reached. Again take the left fork (*do not* take the Parashant Road to the right) to the abandoned settlement of Mt. Trumbull also called Bundyville. You know when you are there by an old schoolhouse at a major intersection. As many as 1,500 people lived here during the 1920's and 1930's. They attempted to farm and raise livestock but the scant rainfall and rocky ground forced most to leave.

At the schoolhouse turn right (west). About 2 miles from the schoolhouse, you will go through a gate (please leave gates as you found them open or closed); keep left. Another mile and another fork; go right this time. In less than a mile you will go through another gate. Turn left (south) along the west side of a fence. After about 4.5 miles, you will pass through another gate. One and a half miles from this gate, you will come to Mule Point Pond. Turn right here onto a road going south. After one-half mile you will pass a small miner's cabin off to the right. The road then drops down into Trail Canyon and deteriorates into a four-wheel drive track. Remember four-wheel drive is necessary to make the *return* trip out of the canyon.

Three miles from Mule Point Pond the road enters the floor of

Parashant Canyon. About 16.5 miles from Mule Point Pond, you reach a major fork. The right fork drops into Andrus Canyon which flows into Parashant. The left fork takes you to the abandoned Copper Mountain Mine. From the wooden cabins, the road descends into a canyon and dead-ends. From here it is only about a half mile to Parashant Canyon.

From here to the Colorado River is about 10 miles and moderate hiking. In June, 1946 Harry Aleson and pioneer river-runner Georgie White Clark hiked about 120 miles from St. George, Utah down Parashant to the river where they donned life preservers and jumped in. The raging Colorado swept them downstream. At times they thought they would drown, but miraculously they reached Lake Mead and were met by a boat.

# GRAND CANYON TRAIL #29

| | |
|---|---|
| Name: | Diamond Creek |
| Trail Location: | #29 on the Index Map |
| Trailhead Elevation: | 1,550 feet |
| Total Vertical Ascent: | Depends on final destination |
| Length (one way): | One to many days |
| Maps: | U.S.G.S. Topos—Diamond Peak; Peach Springs NE |
| Overall Difficulty: | Difficult; route-finding skills necessary |
| Permit: | Hualapai |

Other than Lee's Ferry, Diamond Creek is the only place where you can drive a car to the edge of the Colorado River within the Grand Canyon. As a matter of fact, the first regular tourist stagecoaches came to this spot from the railroad at Peach Springs, some 20 miles to the south. A hotel was built by J.H. Farlee in 1884 at the mouth of Diamond Creek, but by 1889 tourism had shifted to the South Rim area.

Today the road and Diamond Creek are on the Hualapai Indian Reservation and permission must be obtained from the Hualapai Wildlife and Outdoor Recreation Department, P.O. Box 216, Peach Springs, Arizona 86434; (602) 769-2227.

The dirt and gravel road takes off from the north side of Peach Springs and travels down Peach Springs Canyon. The road is usually passable by any high clearance auto or truck, although heavy rains occasionally produce washouts. The Hualapais usually quickly grade the road since this is a common exit route for many of the Colorado River runners.

About 20 miles from Peach Springs (and about 1 mile from the Colorado River), a large canyon on the right (east) comes in from which Diamond Creek emerges. From here to the Colorado, the road more or less follows the stream.

Several hiking options exist. None follow established trails and all require previous canyon hiking experience and knowledge of map and compass. The excellent 7.5-minute topo quads available for western Grand Canyon are a joy to use; topographic detail is fantastic.

One hiking trip would be to follow Diamond Creek upstream

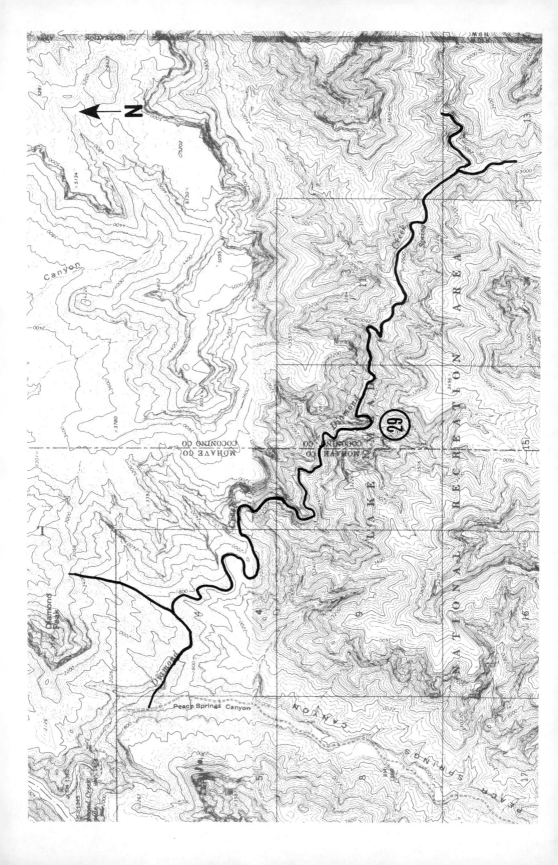

through the Precambrian schist. About .75 miles from the junction of the road and the creek there is a drainage to the north leading to the saddle east of Diamond Peak. Some scrambling is necessary. From the saddle head eastward to the top of the Tapeats Sandstone which is forming the Tonto Platform. Once the Tonto Platform is reached, extended trips to Granite Springs Canyon (about 6 miles from the trailhead) and beyond are possible.

As usual, water is scarce although there are a few seeps and seasonal streams in some of the major side canyons. This area should be avoided during the summer season.

Another trip would involve following Diamond Creek into its upper reaches. There are some route-finding problems though. In 1973 a huge flood created a deep, cold pool in a narrow part of the canyon. If you look at the Diamond Peak Quad, this pool was located about where the "k" is in the work creek.

Other floods since then have no doubt rearranged things. But if you can find ways around (or if it is warm enough to wade or swim through) these pools, the narrows soon give way to a more open valley. Another obstacle along this narrow stretch is a jungle of salt cedar and willows unless a recent flood has scoured the canyon.

About 5 miles from the trailhead, you will come to a major fork. The left fork is Diamond Creek; the right fork is Blue Mountain Canyon (shown as Robbers' Roost Canyon on other maps). Both canyons are carved out of Redwall Limestone and are delightful.

Each canyon contains small groves of cottonwood trees. This is a good area for observing bighorn sheep, mountain lion, and mule deer. "Wild" horses roam over this part of the Hualapai Reservation.

The prehistoric Cohonina Indians left behind arrowheads, a little pottery, and an occasional mescal pit—a circular hole in the ground where they would roast agave or century plants.

Hikers in Western Grand Canyon

David Hubbard

# GRAND CANYON TRAIL #30

**Name:** Routes in Western Grand Canyon

The remote, wild country of the western end of the Grand Canyon offers hardcore backpackers and explorers some tremendous possibilities. Just reaching the rim can be an epic adventure.

The Hualapai Indian Reservation occupies the south rim and permits must be obtained from them. The north rim is under national park service jurisdiction and is probably one of the least visited areas in the Southwest. Sturdy, four-wheel drive vehicles, extra gas, water, tools, and food are necessary to explore this region. Roger Mitchell's book, *Grand Canyon Jeep Trails 1, North Rim*, is helpful in locating roads. And Harvey Butchart's *Grand Canyon Treks II* briefly discusses some hiking possibilities. He is currently working on a *Grand Canyon Treks III* that promises to contain adventurous routes into western Grand Canyon.

# Further Reading

Aitchison, Stewart, "Elve's Chasm," *Summit* (1968), 14(10):2–5.

Aitchison, Stewart, "A Grand Canyon Trek Around the Thumb," *Summit* (1975), 21(7):10–13.

Aitchison, Stewart, "Human Impact on the Grand Canyon," *Down River* (1976), 3(2):18–19.

Aitchison, Stewart, "The Grand Canyon Is a World in Itself," *Plateau* (1977), 49(4):3–9.

Aitchison, Stewart, "Footprints in the Canyon," *Summit* (1982), 28(6):11–14.

Anthony, H.E., "The Facts About Shiva," *Natural History*, December (1937), 709–776.

Babbitt, Bruce, *Grand Canyon Anthology* (1978), Northland Press, Flagstaff, Arizona.

Berkowitz, Alan, *Guide to the Bright Angel Trail* (1979), Grand Canyon Natural History Association, Grand Canyon.

Berkowitz, Alan, *Guide to the North Kaibab Trail* (1980), Grand Canyon Natural History Association, Grand Canyon.

Breed, William and Evelyn Roat, eds, *Geology of the Grand Canyon* (1974), Museum of Northern Arizona, Flagstaff, Arizona.

Brown, Bryan, et al., *Birds of the Grand Canyon Region: An Annotated Checklist* (1978), Grand Canyon Natural History Association, Grand Canyon.

Burroughs, John, "The Grand Cañon of the Colorado," *Century Magazine* (1911), LXXXI:425–438.

Butchart, Harvey, "Old Trails in the Grand Canyon," *Appalachia* (1962), 28(7):45–64.

Butchart, Harvey, "Backpacking Grand Canyon Trails," *Summit* (1964), 10(5):12–19.

Butchart, Harvey, "Routes into Grand Canyon's Remote Upper Corner," *Summit* (1968), 14(2):22–28.

Butchart, Harvey, *Grand Canyon Treks* (1970), La Siesta Press, Glendale, California.

Butchart, Harvey, "Grand Canyon's Enfilade Point Route," *Summit* (1973), 19(5):18–21.

Butchart, Harvey, *Grand Canyon Treks II* (1975), La Siesta Press, Glendale, California.

Butchart, Harvey, "Summits Below the Rim," *The Journal of Arizona History* (1976), 17(1):21–38.

Carothers, Steven, et al., *History and Bibliography of Biological Research in the Grand Canyon Region with an Emphasis on the Riparian Zone* (1974), Unpublished NPS Report, Grand Canyon, Arizona.

Carothers, Steven and Stewart Aitchison, eds, *An Ecological Survey of the Riparian Zone* (1976), Colorado River Research Series, Technical Report No. 10, National Park Service, Grand Canyon, Arizona.

Collier, Michael, *An Introduction to Grand Canyon Geology* (1980), Grand Canyon Natural History Association, Grand Canyon, Arizona.

Coues, Elliott, *Birds of the Colorado Valley* (1878), Government Printing Office, Washington, D.C.

Crampton, C. Gregory, *Land of Living Rock* (1972), A.A. Knopf, New York, New York.

Crumbo, Kim, *A River Runner's Guide to the History of the Grand Canyon* (1981), Johnson Books, Boulder, Colorado.

Dellenbaugh, Frederick, *The Romance of the Colorado River* (1902), G. P. Putnam's Sons, New York, New York.

Dutton, Clarence, *Tertiary History of the Grand Cañon District, with Atlas* (1882), Monographs of the U.S. Geological Survey, Government Printing Office, Washington, D.C.

Fletcher, Colin, "Backpacking the Grand Canyon," *Field and Stream* (1964), March.

Fletcher, Colin, *The Man Who Walked Through Time* (1967), A.A. Knopf, New York, New York.

Freeman, Lewis, *Down the Grand Canyon* (1924), Dodd, Mead and Company, New York, New York.

Ganci, Dave, *Hiking the Desert* (1979), Contemporary Books, Inc., Chicago, Illinois.

Hamblin, W. Kenneth and Joseph Murphy, *Grand Canyon Perspectives* (1969), Brigham Young University, Provo, Utah.

Hirst, Stephen, *Life in a Narrow Place* (1976), David McKay Company, New York, New York.

Hoffmeister, Donald, *Mammals of the Grand Canyon* (1971), University of Illinois Press, Urbana, Illinois.

Hughes, Donald, *In the House of Stone and Light* (1978), Grand Canyon Natural History Association, Grand Canyon, Arizona.

Ives, Joseph, *Report Upon the Colorado River of the West: Explored in 1857 and 1858* (1861), Government Printing Office, Washington, D.C.

James, George, *In and Around the Grand Canyon* (1900), Little, Brown and Company, Boston, Massachusetts.

James, George, *The Grand Canyon of Arizona: How to See It* (1910), Little, Brown and Company, Boston, Massachusetts.

Jones, Anne and Robert Euler, *A Sketch of Grand Canyon Prehistory* (1979), Grand Canyon Natural History Association, Grand Canyon, Arizona.

McKee, Edwin D., *Ancient Landscapes of the Grand Canyon Region* (1931), Northland Press, Flagstaff, Arizona.

Merriam, C. Hart, "Results of a Biological Survey of the San Francisco Mountain Region and Desert of the Little Colorado, Arizona," *North American Fauna #3* (1890), U.S.D.A., Washington, D.C.

Mitchell, Roger, *Grand Canyon Jeep Trails I* (1977), La Siesta Press, Glendale, California.

Peattie, Roderick, ed, *The Inverted Mountains: Canyons of the West* (1948), Vanguard Press, New York, New York.

Phillips, Arthur, *Grand Canyon Wildflowers* (1979), Grand Canyon Natural History Association, Grand Canyon, Arizona.

Powell, John W., *Exploration of the Colorado River of the West and Its Tributaries* (1895), U.S. Government Printing Office, Washington, D.C., Reprinted by Dover Publications (1961), New York, New York.

Rusho, W.L. and C. Gregory Crampton, *Desert River Crossing* (1975), Peregrine Smith, Salt Lake City, Utah.

Simmons, Virginia, "Dry Trail to Thunder Spring," *Summit* (1976), 22(1):28–33.

Simpson, Elizabeth, *Recollections of Phantom Ranch* (1979), Grand Canyon Natural History Association, Grand Canyon, Arizona.

Stanton, Robert, *Down the Colorado* (1965), University of Oklahoma Press, Norman, Oklahoma.

Sterling, K.B., *Last of the Naturalists: The Career of C. Hart Merriam* (1974), Arno Press, New York, New York.

Stone, Julius, *Canyon Country* (1932), G.P. Putnam's Sons, New York, New York.

Sutton, Ann and Myron Sutton, *The Wilderness World of the Grand Canyon* (1971), Lippincott, Philadelphia, Pennsylvania.

Thybony, Scott, *A Guide to Hiking the Inner Canyon* (1980), Grand Canyon Natural History Association, Grand Canyon, Arizona.

Ullman, James, *Down the Colorado with Major Powell* (1960), Houghton Mifflin Co., Boston, Massachusetts.

Wampler, Joseph, *Havasu Canyon* (1959), Wampler, Berkeley, California.

Whitney, Stephen, *A Field Guide to the Grand Canyon* (1982), William Morrow and Co., New York, New York.

Wilkerson, James, ed, *Medicine for Mountaineering* (1975), The Mountaineers, Seattle, Washington.

# Author's Biography

*Stewart Aitchison is a naturalist and guide for several outdoor adventure/educational outfitters. He has authored numerous scientific and popular articles as well as the books* Oak Creek Canyon and the Red Rock Country of Arizona *and* A Naturalist's San Juan River Guide. *He lives a passive solar-life with his wife, Ann, in Flagstaff, Arizona.*